Highly Sensitive Empath

vs.

Narcissistic Individual Decoded

A Comprehensive Guide to Recognize, Navigate, and Flourish in Relationships with These Contrasting Personalities

Joyce T

Table of Contents

INTRODUCTION

Before anything, we have to make one thing clear – it wasn't your fault.

You did not deserve the abuse.

"Being soft" or "being too nice" is not your fault, and it's certainly not a bad thing.

You are an empath, and you just happened to cross paths with a narcissist who didn't appreciate your strengths – because this is what they are.

A few years back, I was in the same situation as you are or have been in. I'd be lying if I said that wasn't one of the hardest and darkest periods of my life. I felt unseen, unheard, not understood, underappreciated, and absolutely not myself. If you've been in a relationship with a narcissist, then you can understand what this can do to a person.

But don't worry; you can understand yourself and the empath-narcissist relationship dynamic better and eventually find yourself once again.

Throughout the book, I'll be sharing my experiences with you, and I hope that this gives you some practical perspective that will shed a deeper light on what it means to be a highly sensitive empath and how you relate to others and the world.

For now, let me give you a little backstory so that you can understand where I'm coming from. I met my first love when I was 19 years old. We all know there's nothing more infatuating than young love. Joshua (not his real name for privacy purposes, but I'll be using this name throughout the book) made me feel like I was over the moon. He made me feel like I was the only girl in the world and that we would spend the rest of our lives together. But this feeling only lasted in the initial months and intermittently through the 5 years we were together.

I say intermittently because with a narcissist, they will constantly build you up so that they can break you down, and when they do, they will build you back up again, and the cycle continues. If I were to summarize the five years with Joshua, I can say that it was the most toxicity I have ever experienced in life, and as you continue reading this book, you will understand why.

Why does this book matter, you may ask? Well, dear reader, because it's about you! It's about the relationships you're in, as well as the people you encounter daily and how you navigate through these interactions. It's about offering you knowledge and strategies to do more than survive and flourish in your relationships.

We will take a two-fold approach: evidence-based and empathy-driven. Over the years, I have learned that real understanding comes from a balance between factual information and emotional connection. In our shared journey throughout this book, we will lean on respected research to guide our factual understanding as well as rely heavily on empathy to understand the unique personalities of empaths and narcissists.

Remember, this isn't just a book; it's a step toward exploring, learning, and growing, and I'll be right here with you every step of the way.

So, let's turn the page and begin our journey together!

Chapter 1

THE EMPATH: PORTRAIT OF SENSITIVITY

1

Did you know that some people can feel others' emotions as if they were their own? It might seem like a plot from a sci-fi movie, but it is the reality for those identified as empaths.

Before we dive into the dynamics of empaths and narcissist relationships, it's important first to understand yourself as an empath.

1.1 The Empath Defined

Empaths, often referred to as 'emotional sponges,' are individuals who can absorb and intuit other people's emotions. as an empath, your heightened sensitivity to others' feelings and moods is what sets you apart.

As we will discover, this capability to tune into the emotional undercurrents around you can be both a blessing and a curse.

Emotional Sponges

Think back to the last time you were in a crowded room. Recall the chatter, the energy, and the varying moods. Now, imagine if you could feel all those emotions and energy as if they were your own. That is how it is for empaths. You can walk into a room and get a sense of the emotional climate.

You can sit next to a friend who has just had a terrible day and start to feel down or upset, too, even if our day was perfectly fine. The ability to absorb emotions from others is the reason why empaths are described as emotional sponges.

High Sensitivity to Environment

Beyond emotions alone, as an empath, you exhibit high sensitivity to your environment. You may pick up on subtle changes in the atmosphere, noise level, or energy in a room. At times, this sensitivity can be overwhelming.

You know the feeling when you're trying to focus, but there is a TV on in the background? That is how everyday life can be for an empath. You constantly pick up on small signals around you, making it challenging to tune out background noise and focus on your needs and feelings.

In light of this, you can understand how hard it can be to focus on your needs and feelings when those of a narcissist are always the loudest.

Deep Understanding of Others' Emotions

The third defining trait of an empath is their deep understanding of others' emotions. Since you feel what others are feeling, empaths often understand emotions on a profound level. It is a trait that makes some empaths excellent listeners, supportive friends, or compassionate partners. You can provide comfort in times of distress, as you truly understand the emotional experiences of the person that you are comforting.

Take, for instance, a situation where a friend has just gone through a devastating breakup. Many people will offer supportive words or try to distract their friend from the pain, but an empath will truly feel the heartache and loss that their friend is experiencing. You can sit with your friend in that emotional space, providing understanding and comfort in a way that few others can.

It is important to note that being an empath is not about simply being very empathetic or compassionate—while those are wonderful traits that many empaths possess, being an empath is more than that: it is about feeling and understanding emotions on a deep, intuitive level.

Although it is also important to note that individual empaths' experiences vary. As with other aspects of personality and human nature, empathy exists on a spectrum. This means that some people might identify as being slightly empathetic, while others may feel that they are highly empathetic.

Understanding the traits of an empath is just the first step. As we explore further, we will look at the different types of empaths, delve into the unique abilities that empaths possess, and share some strategies for managing these abilities in a healthy, beneficial way.

1.2 The Empath Spectrum: From Highly Sensitive to Ultra-empathic

We have established that empathy exists on a spectrum, that it is not a one-size-fits-all attribute but rather a continuum of experiences and abilities. At one end of the spectrum, we find highly sensitive individuals. At the other end, we have ultra-empathic individuals, each with their own unique experiences and challenges.

Let's explore this spectrum more closely.

Highly Sensitive People

The highly sensitive person, or HSP, represents the milder end of the empathic spectrum. They are often profoundly affected by the physical and emotional environments around them. For example, they might be moved by a beautiful piece of music, feel overwhelmed in crowded spaces, or pick up on subtle shifts in a friend's mood.

While all empaths are sensitive to some degree, not all highly sensitive individuals are empaths. The key difference lies in the depth of emotional absorption: highly sensitive individuals are attuned to the feelings and moods of others and their environment but, crucially, do not necessarily absorb and experience these emotions as their own.

Emotional Empaths

As we progress along the spectrum, we find emotional empaths. These individuals do not only sense the emotions of others; they actually feel them. If a friend is feeling anxious, it could feel like it rubs off on the emotional empath. If a family member is sad, the emotional empath could feel a wave of sadness wash over them.

This emotional mirroring can be both a blessing and a curse. On the one hand, it allows emotional empaths to connect deeply with others, providing comfort and understanding on a profound level. On the other hand, it can be emotionally draining, especially when the feelings being absorbed are negative or intense.

Intuitive Empaths

Further along the spectrum, intuitive empaths are waiting for us. These individuals have a strong sense of 'knowing' that goes beyond simply feeling the emotions of others. They might have a gut feeling about a situation or a person that turns out to be accurate. They might know how someone is feeling even before that person has fully processed their own emotions.

This intuitive ability can be a powerful tool, as it can guide decision-making, enhance relationships, and act as a form of self-protection. The downside is that it can be overwhelming at times, especially when the intuitive empath is picking up on negative or confusing signals.

Telepathic Empaths

The far end of the empathic spectrum is represented by telepathic empaths. These individuals can pick up on others' thoughts and feelings even if they are not expressed. It is almost like mind reading, although sensing the energy of thoughts and emotions rather than hearing them word for word.

Telepathic empathy is a rare and powerful ability. It can foster deep connections and understanding, and it can be a source of insight and wisdom. However, it can also be challenging to manage, especially when the telepathic empath is picking up on a lot of mental chatter or negative thoughts.

While this categorization can help us understand the broad range of empathic sensations, it is important to remember that each empath's experience is unique. Some might identify with aspects of all these categories, while others might resonate strongly with just one.

Understanding where you fall on the empathic spectrum is a crucial step in learning how to navigate your empathic abilities. It can help you identify your strengths, recognize challenges, and find the strategies that work best for you. So, take a moment to reflect on which of these categories resonates most with you.

Remember, there is no right or wrong answer. It is about identifying what feels true for you, and that truth is what will guide you as we continue to explore the world of empaths.

1.3 Empathic Abilities: A Deeper Look

You have probably heard the phrase, "with great power comes great responsibility." This could not be more accurate for empaths. You have a unique set of abilities, which are sometimes challenging to manage but can be used for the incredible good. Let's explore these abilities in more detail.

Emotional Healing

With your deep understanding of emotions, you can often help others process and heal from emotional pain. If a friend who's just experienced a painful breakup is heartbroken, confused, and perhaps angry, they might seem inconsolable to most.

The empath: sitting with their friend, listening to their pain and truly feeling it, they offer comfort from a place of understanding, not just sympathy. In validating your friend's feelings, you make them feel seen and understood. This act of validation can be incredibly healing and help process emotions rather than pushing them away.

Intuition

Empaths often have a strong sense of intuition. Sometimes, your gut feeling about a person or situation turns out to be exactly right. This intuition can serve as a kind of internal compass, guiding you toward positive experiences and away from potentially harmful situations.

Consider, for example, a job interview where the interviewer is friendly, the office is beautiful, and the job seems perfect. But something feels off. You can't quite put your finger on it, but you trust your intuition and decide to turn down the job offer. Later, you find out that the company was hiding a host of issues, from poor management to unethical practices. In this case, following your intuition protected you.

Energy Perception

Another unique ability of empaths is energy perception. Sensing the 'vibe' or energy of a person, a place, or even an object is more than just picking up on mood or atmosphere; it is about sensing the subtle energetic frequencies that everything in our universe emits.

Maybe you have been in a situation where you walk into a room after an argument has taken place, and despite no one having told you about the argument, you feel the tension in the air, a looming heaviness. That sensation exemplifies energy perception. For empaths, this ability is often much more nuanced. They might sense a wide range of energies, from the calming energy of a forest to the frantic energy of a busy city street.

Animal Communication

Last but not least, some empaths have a unique connection with animals and can sense their emotions and needs in a way that most humans can't. This ability can range from simply understanding an animal's basic needs to actually sensing the animal's emotions and thoughts.

To exemplify again, imagine a dog shelter. One of the dogs is terrified, confused, and desperately wants to be loved. Most people are able to see a dog in distress, but an empath can feel the dog's fear, confusion, and longing. They can provide comfort and understanding in a way that the dog desperately needs. This ability can be incredibly beneficial in fields like animal rescue, pet training, or even veterinary medicine.

These abilities—emotional healing, intuition, energy perception, and animal communication—are what make empaths so unique. They allow you to connect with the world around you in a deep, meaningful way.

As was mentioned, however, they can also be overwhelming at times. In the following chapters, we will discuss strategies to manage these abilities in a healthy, beneficial way. For now, take some time to reflect on these abilities. Do any of them resonate with you? If so, how might you use them in a positive, empowering way? Remember, your empathic abilities are not a burden, but a gift—a gift that allows you to connect, understand, and heal in a way that few others can.

1.4 Personal Stories: Life as an Empath

Empathy is a complex and multifaceted trait, and no two empaths experience it in exactly the same way. To give you a better understanding of what it is like to live as an empath, I have collected a few real-life examples, which I'm going to share with you.

These stories highlight the triumphs and everyday struggles that empaths face and offer insights into how they manage their unique abilities.

Overcoming Emotional Overwhelmingness

Shopping malls during the holiday season are one thing: festively chaotic. Picture the chatter of hundreds of shoppers, the blare of festive music, the pressure of finding the perfect gift—it's an environment that can overwhelm anyone. But for Sarah, who was an empath, it was almost unbearable.

Sarah would absorb all the stress, excitement, and impatience around her until it felt like a crushing weight. It was exhausting and often left her feeling drained and emotionally raw. But over time, Sarah found ways to cope.

She began practicing grounding techniques, like focusing on her breath or the feeling of her feet on the floor. She started carrying a small object (a smooth, cool stone) that she could touch whenever she felt overwhelmed. This helped her to center herself and create a sense of calm amidst the chaos.

Sarah's experience is common among empaths. The emotional noise of the world is often overwhelming, but like Sarah, you can employ strategies to ground yourself and create a sense of calm in your inner world when the outer world is in turmoil.

Navigating Relationships

Being an empath can also have a profound impact on relationships. A guy named Mark, for example, had empathic abilities that made him an exceptional friend and partner. He could sense when his loved ones were upset, even if they tried to hide it. He could provide comfort and understanding in a way that few others could. However, his relationships were also a source of challenge.

Mark often found himself taking on his partner's emotions and problems as his own. He would become so absorbed in their feelings that he would lose sight of his own needs. This led to a pattern of one-sided relationships where Mark was always the giver, and his partners were always the takers.

Eventually, Mark learned to set boundaries in his relationships. He realized that he could be there for his loved ones without taking on their emotions as his own. He learned to differentiate between his feelings and theirs. This allowed him to be a supportive partner and friend without sacrificing his own emotional well-being.

Harnessing Empathic Abilities for Good

Finally, the story of Lily. Lily always knew that she was different. She could sense things that others could not. She could feel the emotions of the people around her, and she had a deep, intuitive understanding of their experiences. For a long time, she considered this a burden, as it made her feel different and often left her overwhelmed and drained.

Over time, Lily began to see her empathic abilities in a new light. She saw how her empathy allowed her to connect with others on a deep level. She saw how it made her a better friend, a better sister, a better daughter. She saw how it could be used to make a positive impact in the world.

Lily became a counselor, using her empathic abilities to help others navigate their emotional landscape. She used her deep understanding of emotions to guide her clients toward healing and self-understanding. What was once a heavy burden she turned into her greatest strength.

Each of these stories highlights a different aspect of life as an empath. They illustrate the challenges that empaths often face, from emotional overwhelmingness to one-sided relationships and overall struggles. However, they also show the incredible potential of empathic abilities and how you can learn to manage and use them to your advantage.

Think about your own empathetic abilities. How can you use them to your advantage?

____

____

____

____

____

____

____

As we move forward, we will further explore the world of empaths and narcissists. We will delve into strategies for managing empathic abilities, setting boundaries, and navigating relationships with narcissists. But for now, let these stories serve as a reminder that being an empath, even though a little difficult, comes with incredible potential, deep connections, and the ability to impact the world and others' lives positively.

Chapter 2

THE NARCISSIST: A STUDY IN SELF-ADORATION

2

When I was dating my ex, Joshua, I will always remember how much he loved attention and admiration – from me or anyone who would give it to him.

A few years into our relationship, we attended my sister's baby shower. Thankfully, gone are the days when men attending baby showers is seen as a "taboo." It was a simple function with family only, and we got there a little early so that I could help out with the preparations.

As you would imagine, I had my plate full, and so did most of the people there. I glanced at him a few times from the kitchen and noticed that he sat by himself in a corner, going through his phone, looking a little bit too serious for a baby shower.

I heard my brother ask him to help hang a banner that needed him to climb a small ladder, and he blatantly said that he would rather not climb on a ladder. After hearing this, I approached him and asked if everything was okay, and he said yes without even looking at me. He remained the same for the rest of the event, and I remember at one point, my sister asked me if Joshua was fine.

This didn't make any sense. We had been to a few of his family's events and his own birthday parties, and Joshua was always the highlight of the party, talking and laughing with people. But come to think of it, the subject matter was always him in those conversations.

During the car ride back home, I pushed him to tell me what was wrong and why he acted the way he did.

He said, "I don't understand why you would leave me by myself and go hang out with your family in the kitchen."

I was a little taken aback because he knew that I was in there cooking, and I had introduced him to my brother, who was in the living room with him. I told him this, and he said, "You made me feel alone, and I didn't like that. You should learn to be more considerate."

I felt guilty, apologized to him, and reassured him that wasn't my intention. But that wasn't the last time I heard that statement.

Narcissists thrive on attention and admiration, and when they lack it, they can feel starved and turn into someone different.

This is the essence of narcissism, and it's the individual we are about to understand better.

2.1 Narcissism Unveiled

When we delve into the world of narcissism, we encounter a complex landscape of behaviors and attitudes. Three key attributes stand out prominently in a narcissist: an inflated sense of self-importance (grandiosity), a lack of empathy for others, and a strong need for admiration.

Grandiosity

Think about someone who always seems to make the conversation about them or someone who consistently exaggerates their achievements and abilities. These are signs of grandiosity, a key trait of narcissism.

Grandiosity can manifest in various ways, from boastfulness and arrogance to an entitlement mentality. Narcissists believe that they are deserving of special treatment and that they are superior to others—beliefs that they are not shy about expressing.

I always say that you leave a narcissist countless times before actually leaving them. I remember during one of these instances when I told Joshua that I was going to leave him, he told me that he was an amazing man and I would never find anyone else like him. The most astonishing part is that he truly believed this.

Lack of Empathy

While grandiosity is a visible trait of narcissism, lack of empathy is more subtle yet equally significant. Empathy, as we've explored, is the ability to understand and share others' feelings. It's what allows us to connect on a deep, emotional level. For narcissists, this quality is noticeably absent.

Narcissists struggle to put themselves in others' shoes and to consider others' feelings. They may dismiss or diminish others' needs and emotions, focusing predominantly on their own. It is akin to someone wearing noise-canceling headphones in a bustling café; they're in the same space as everyone else, but they're detached, engrossed in their own world, oblivious to the experiences of those around them.

For instance, if a friend is sharing about a challenging day they've had, a narcissist might dismiss their feelings or quickly steer the conversation back to themselves. They might say something like, "Well, you think your day was bad? Let me tell you about mine!" This lack of empathy can make interactions with a narcissist feel one-sided and emotionally unsatisfying.

In my past relationship with Joshua, I always felt like when I shared something, it was a competition. If I told him that sometimes I felt he didn't understand me, he would switch it up and tell me it's because I never understood him.

If I told him about something difficult in my past, he would counter it with something from his own past. Even if I told him about something good I had seen or heard, he would make sure to steer the topic to his own experience. It was like he never even heard me.

Need for Admiration

The third pillar of narcissism is a strong need for admiration. Narcissists crave admiration, like plants crave sunlight. They thrive on validation and praise from others, seeking it out to maintain their inflated self-image.

A façade of confidence and self-assuredness often masks this need for admiration. However, beneath the surface lies a fragile self-esteem that depends heavily on external validation. When this validation is not forthcoming, a narcissist may react with anger, impatience, or attempts to belittle others to boost their own self-worth.

Think of someone who constantly posts carefully curated images of their life on social media, fishing for likes and comments. Or someone who reacts defensively to even the slightest criticism, turning it around to highlight their own achievements or diminish the accomplishments of others. These are common scenarios where a narcissist's need for admiration becomes evident.

Understanding these key traits of narcissism—grandiosity, a lack of empathy, and a need for admiration—provides a crucial lens to recognize and interpret narcissistic behaviors. With this lens, you are better equipped to navigate interactions with narcissistic individuals and to protect your emotional well-being.

2.2 The Narcissist Spectrum: From Healthy Self-love to Pathological Narcissism

Just as the empath's experience exists on a spectrum, so does the narcissist's. Narcissism isn't a one-size-fits-all term. It unfolds along a range from healthy self-love to pathological narcissism. Understanding this spectrum is akin to understanding the different shades of a color. Each shade is unique and distinct, yet they all belong to the same color family.

Healthy Narcissism

At one end of the spectrum, we find healthy narcissism. It's like the lightest shade of our color, barely noticeable but still present. Healthy narcissism is essentially a balanced sense of self-love and self-esteem. It's about appreciating your own worth, setting healthy boundaries, and taking pride in your accomplishments.

Think of someone who stands up for themselves in a difficult situation or takes the time to celebrate their achievements. This is healthy narcissism in action. It's self-assured, confident, and positive. It doesn't involve belittling others to feel good about oneself. Instead, it's about recognizing and respecting one's own worth.

Malignant Narcissism

As we move along the spectrum, the shade of our color becomes darker and more pronounced. We enter the territory of malignant narcissism. This is where the traits we discussed earlier—grandiosity, lack of empathy, and need for admiration—start to manifest in harmful ways.

For example, often disregarding the feelings and needs of others, manipulating and exploiting people to serve the narcissists' own ends, and they may display aggressive or antisocial behaviors. Imagine a coworker who takes credit for your ideas, or a partner who belittles you to boost their own ego. These are glimpses of malignant narcissism.

Despite their outward display of confidence, individuals in which malignant narcissism can be found often harbor fragile self-esteem. They rely heavily on external validation to maintain their inflated self-image. Without constant admiration and attention, they may feel threatened or insecure.

Narcissistic Personality Disorder

At the far end of the spectrum, we encounter the darkest shade of our color: Narcissistic Personality Disorder (NPD). This is a clinically diagnosed mental condition characterized by persistent patterns of grandiosity, a profound need for admiration, and a striking lack of empathy.

Individuals with NPD often have a distorted self-image. They perceive themselves as superior, exceptional, or unique. They believe that they deserve special treatment and that ordinary rules don't apply to them. They may become angry or distressed when they don't receive the admiration that they feel they deserve.

It is important to note that NPD goes beyond simply being self-centered or vain. It is a serious disorder that can cause significant distress and impairment. Those with NPD often struggle with relationships, work, school, and their sense of identity. They may also experience other mental health issues, such as depression, anxiety, or substance abuse.

From the above types of narcissists, which kind have you ever come across?

____

____

____

____

____

____

Understanding the narcissism spectrum is like having a map to navigate the complex landscape of narcissistic behaviors. It allows us to recognize the varying shades of narcissism and to respond appropriately.

Whether dealing with healthy self-love or pathological narcissism, having this map can equip us to protect our emotional well-being and foster healthier interactions with those on the narcissism spectrum.

2.3 Narcissistic Behaviors: Recognizing the Signs

The world of a narcissist is a fascinating one to examine. As we've seen, it's marked by grandiosity, a distinct lack of empathy, and a relentless pursuit of admiration.

Underpinning these characteristics is a suite of behaviors that are commonly exhibited by those with a narcissistic personality. Let's turn our attention to some of these behaviors: gaslighting, love bombing, and hoovering.

Love Bombing

Joshua and I met as coworkers when I was 19. If I'm being honest, I wasn't initially attracted to him right off the bat. He wasn't exactly very attractive, nor was he successful, but he had this charm and sense of humor that really stood out. There was just something about him that was attractive, even though I couldn't quite put a finger on it.

Our first year together was like a dream. The spontaneous dates, a healthy supply of affection, tenderness, and respect made me feel like I had found my "Mr. Right." But shortly after the honeymoon stage was over, I came to discover that he was cheating on me the whole time – since the very first day. He had actually been with the other person for a couple of years and had promised to marry her soon.

When I found out and confronted him, he made excuses that actually made sense at the time. He said that he didn't really love her and that he felt obligated to be with her because she had been helping him all these years.

Love bombing often serves as a smokescreen, masking the narcissist's true intentions while winning over their target. The narcissist creates a powerful emotional bond, making their partner feel special and loved. However, this intense affection often fades as quickly as it appears, which leaves the partner confused and craving the affection they once received.

Narcissists use love bombing to establish control and manipulate their partners. Once the love bombing phase is over, they may start to devalue their partner or use the established emotional bond to control and manipulate them.

Gaslighting

Picture a scenario where you're certain that your friend promised to help you with a project this weekend. But when you remind them, they deny ever making such a promise. You're left feeling bewildered, doubting your own memory. This is a classic example of gaslighting—a manipulative tactic often employed by narcissists.

Gaslighting involves twisting the truth, denying facts, and creating doubt in others to control or manipulate them. The term originates from a 1944 film called Gaslight, where a husband manipulates his wife into believing that she's losing her sanity. In real life, gaslighting can be just as disorientating.

Joshua cheated on me over and over again, and every time, he made me feel like I was hallucinating and that everything was my fault. I remember hearing him talking to a woman on the phone one time after coming to the house in the middle of the night. He told her he had a good time and got back safely.

Joshua thought I was asleep, and when I asked him the next day, he said that it was his male friend he was hanging out with, and I didn't know what I was talking about. I had clearly heard a female voice on the other end, and he started making me feel like I had hallucinated it.

You might find a narcissist using gaslighting to evade responsibility, make you question your perceptions, or make themselves appear superior. Over time, this can lead to confusion, anxiety, and a crippling loss of self-confidence.

Hoovering

Named after the famous brand of vacuum cleaners, the act of hoovering refers to the narcissist's attempts to suck their victims back into a relationship. This behavior usually occurs after a breakup or period of separation. The narcissist uses promises, flattery, or even threats to reel their partner back in.

Hoovering can be confusing and emotionally draining. One moment, the narcissist is showering their ex-partner with affection, pleading for a second chance; the next, they use guilt-tripping or threats to manipulate them into returning.

During the times we broke up with Joshua, he would even send me sweet little handwritten notes, and if I didn't respond positively, the next day, he used threats to persuade me back. These would read something like, "After all that we have been through, you are just going to throw everything in the trash like we were nothing?"

It's important to note that hoovering is not about the narcissist's love for their partner. Rather, it's about their desire for control and their fear of abandonment. They view their partner as a source of narcissistic supply—admiration, validation, and attention—and use manipulative tactics to keep the supply from running out.

Isolation

After Joshua begged me to forgive him for cheating, things went downhill from there. The relationship got very toxic as he started being extremely jealous of all the guy friends I had, including a gay friend I was very close to.

He gave me a hard choice: it was either him or my friends. It was like both could not coexist. I became antisocial and didn't have any life besides him and the toxic life we were building.

Isolation is done in a bid to have full control of you. They don't want other people to "taint" your perception of them because, deep down, they have an idea that some things they do are simply not right.

Recognizing these behaviors—gaslighting, love bombing, isolation, and hoovering—is an essential step in understanding and dealing with narcissistic individuals. Awareness of these tactics can empower you to set boundaries, seek support, and protect your emotional well-being so that the next time you encounter these behaviors, you'll be able to say, "I see what you're doing, and I won't fall for it."

Let's do a little self-reflection:

From the above characteristic traits of a narcissist, which ones have you encountered, and how did they affect you?

____

____

____

____

____

____

____

____

____

____

2.4 Personal Stories: Life with a Narcissist

Interacting with a narcissist can feel like navigating a labyrinth full of twists, turns, and dead ends. Each person's experience in this labyrinth is unique, their path shaped by their own strengths, vulnerabilities, and circumstances.

Besides my own recounts, read through the stories of these three individuals who found themselves in the same situation as me and found their way out.

Surviving Gaslighting

Meet Hannah, a vibrant woman with a strong sense of self. Hannah was in a relationship with Josh, a charismatic man who always seemed to be the life of the party. However, behind closed doors, Josh had a knack for twisting reality in a way that left Hannah questioning her own sanity.

One particular incident stands out in her memory. Hannah had prepared a home-cooked meal for Josh's birthday. She had spent hours planning and cooking, but when Josh arrived, he seemed annoyed. He claimed Hannah had forgotten his dislike for mushrooms, which were a key ingredient in the dish she had lovingly prepared. Hannah was confused; she could not recall him ever mentioning a dislike for mushrooms, but Josh adamantly accused her of not paying attention to his preferences.

This was one of many similar incidents. Over time, Hannah began to doubt her memory and perception. Only when she confided in a friend, who pointed out the possibility of gaslighting, did she begin to see the manipulation for what it was. Recognizing the gaslighting was the first step in Hannah's journey to reclaim her reality and break free from Josh's manipulation.

Breaking Free from Love Bombing

Next, let's turn to David. David was swept off his feet when he first met Lisa. She showered him with affection and attention, making him feel like the center of her universe. However, Lisa's intense affection soon turned into control and manipulation.

She would bombard David with affectionate messages and calls, insisting he respond immediately. If he failed, Lisa would become upset, accusing him of not caring about her. The constant need for attention and reassurance left David feeling drained and constantly on edge.

When he stumbled upon an article about narcissism, David finally discovered that he was being love-bombed and that Lisa's intense affection was not about love but about control. This realization gave him the courage to break free from her manipulative hold.

Healing from Narcissistic Abuse

Lastly, we meet Rachel. Rachel had been in a relationship with Alex, a man whose charm and confidence quickly turned into control and emotional abuse. Alex would belittle Rachel, making her feel worthless and dependent on him. He would oscillate between periods of intense affection and cruel indifference, leaving Rachel emotionally off-balance.

Rachel spent years under Alex's influence, enduring his emotional abuse. The turning point came when Rachel attended a workshop on emotional health and recognized the signs of narcissistic abuse in her relationship.

Acknowledging the abuse was painful, but it was also the first step toward healing. Rachel sought out a therapist who helped her understand the dynamics of narcissistic abuse and supported her in rebuilding her self-esteem. She also joined a support group, where she met others who had experienced similar situations. Despite the lingering pain, Rachel was on a path to recovery, finding strength in her resilience and comfort in the shared experiences of others.

Isolation

Eve had met Danny on a dating site, and their's was an instant connection. Eve had always been a social butterfly, and she had a good number of friends of all genders. But after meeting Danny and dating him for 3 years, Eve was down to zero friends; the only person she kept close contact with was her sister.

So, when her sister asked her why she no longer communicated with even her best friend, with whom she had been friends for over seven years, Eve realized that Danny had pushed them away and not left much of a choice to her.

His tactics were simple, "You hang out too much with her," "I don't trust him," "You could do better," but some weren't, "It's either him or me."

In the end, she was left with no friends. The realization made her see that her real self was dampened, and she needed to act quickly to get back her life – this prompted cutting ties with Danny and moving to a different city to start a fresh start.

Hannah, David, Eve, and Rachel each found themselves entangled with a narcissist. These individuals' experiences, while unique, share common threads of manipulation and control. However, they also share a thread of resilience and empowerment.

Each of them, in their own time and in their own way, detected the narcissistic behaviors they were subjected to. They sought help, set boundaries, and took steps toward healing. Their stories serve as a reminder that while narcissistic behavior can be confusing and damaging, understanding and resilience can light the path out of the labyrinth.

In the world of empaths and narcissists, knowledge is indeed power. The more we understand these contrasting personalities, the better we are to navigate our interactions. In the next chapter, let's understand why empath-narcissist relationships are so common.

Chapter 3

EMPATHS AND NARCISSISTS: A COMPLEX DANCE

3

3.1 Attraction of Opposites: Why Empaths and Narcissists Gravitate Toward Each Other

In the world of human relationships, it's often said that opposites attract. Think of that old couple in your neighborhood, one chatty and outgoing, the other quiet and reserved. They seem so different, yet they've been happily married for decades. Now, consider the empath and the narcissist. Their personalities are poles apart, yet they, too, are drawn toward each other.

Why is this so?

The Caregiver and the Taker

Imagine a well-tended garden, lush with vibrant flowers and verdant foliage. The gardener, dutiful and attentive, spends hours nurturing the plants, ensuring that they thrive. Now, picture a sunflower in that garden, standing tall, its bright, yellow petals soaking up the sunlight, hogging the lion's share of the gardener's attention.

In this scenario, the empath is the gardener, and the narcissist is the sunflower. Emotionally nurturing by nature, empaths often take on the role of caregivers in their relationships. They are drawn toward those they perceive as needing care or understanding, those they feel they can help or heal. Enter the narcissist. With their need for constant attention and validation, narcissists can appear to empaths as individuals who need their care and understanding. This perceived need can draw the empath toward the narcissist, like a gardener to a wilted plant.

A balanced relationship entails both giving and taking, but a relationship between an empath and a narcissist can easily become one-sided. In their caregiver role, the empath may give too much—too much time, too much energy, too much emotional support. The narcissist, on the other hand, may take too much without giving anything back, not reciprocating the care and understanding that the empath offers. This imbalance can lead to the empath feeling drained and unappreciated while the narcissist continues to demand more attention and validation.

The Healer and the Wounded

Let's switch gears for a moment and step into a classroom. Picture a teacher patiently explaining a difficult concept to a struggling student. The teacher sees potential in the student and is determined to help them succeed. The teacher will give it all it takes to ensure the student succeeds – their time, energy, and even sacrifice their mental wellbeing if necessary.

In this scenario, the empath is the teacher, and the narcissist is the struggling student. Empaths, with their deep understanding of emotions, often take on the role of healers. They sense the emotional wounds and insecurities hidden beneath the narcissist's confident exterior. They believe that they can help the narcissist overcome these inner wounds.

The narcissist, on the other hand, may be drawn to the empath's compassion and understanding. They may see the empath as someone who can soothe their insecurities and boost their ego. This dynamic can create a strong bond between the empath and the narcissist, as the empath strives to heal the narcissist's wounds, and the narcissist leans on the empath for emotional support.

However, this healing dynamic can easily become unhealthy if the empath feels responsible for the narcissist's emotional well-being. The empath may neglect their own emotional needs in their quest to heal the narcissist. The narcissist, meanwhile, may become dependent on the empath for emotional validation, further fueling their narcissistic behaviors.

In conclusion, the mutual attraction between empaths and narcissists can be traced back to their contrasting yet complementary roles. The empath, as the caregiver and healer, is drawn toward the narcissist's perceived need for care and understanding. The narcissist, as the taker and the wounded, is drawn toward the empath's compassion and attention. This dynamic, while initially captivating, can lead to a toxic cycle of emotional imbalance and dependency.

3.2 The Empath-Narcissist Relationship: A Toxic Cycle

The Idealization Phase

Picture a summer day at the beach where everything seems perfect: the sun is shining, the waves are gently lapping at the shore, and there's a sense of peace and contentment in the air. This idyllic scene mirrors the initial phase of an empath-narcissist relationship, known as the idealization phase.

During this phase, the narcissist places the empath on a pedestal, showering them with praise, affection, and attention. The empath, in turn, feels valued and loved. They see the narcissist as charming, attentive, and seemingly in tune with their feelings.

This phase is like a perfectly choreographed dance, with the narcissist leading and the empath willingly following. The narcissist's attention and admiration fulfill the empath's desire to be understood and appreciated, while the empath's caring and understanding nature feeds the narcissist's need for validation. It's a dance that feels harmonious and rewarding, creating a strong bond between the empath and the narcissist.

The Devaluation Phase

Like a sudden thunderstorm on a sunny beach day, this harmonious dance is disrupted as the relationship enters the devaluation phase. In this phase, the narcissist starts to undermine the empath, gradually chipping away at their self-esteem and confidence.

This phase always hits the hardest.

You are left wondering, where did the charming person I met a few years/months ago go?

Did you do something that turned them into the person they've become?

The once charming and attentive narcissist becomes critical and dismissive. They may belittle your feelings, disregard your needs, or manipulate them into doubting your own worth. The empath, who once felt valued and loved, now feels perplexed, hurt, and increasingly insecure.

This phase is like a confusing dance where the steps keep changing, leaving you struggling to keep up. You may try to regain the narcissist's approval, often by giving more of yourself and neglecting your own needs. But no matter how hard you try, the narcissist's approval remains elusive, and the dance becomes more and more exhausting.

The Discard Phase

Finally, the relationship enters the discard phase. Picture the aftermath of the storm, where the once sunny beach is now littered with debris. The sky is still dark, and the air is heavy with tension from the storm that just passed. This is the discard phase, a time of reckoning in the empath-narcissist relationship.

In this phase, the narcissist may decide to end the relationship, often abruptly and without consideration for your feelings. The narcissist's reasons for ending the relationship may be unclear or irrational, leaving you feeling blindsided and confused.

This can leave you feeling discarded and worthless. You may be left questioning your worth, feelings, and sanity. The dance that once felt harmonious now feels like a cruel game, leaving you exhausted and emotionally wounded.

In conclusion, the empath-narcissist relationship often follows a predictable cycle: the idealization phase, the devaluation phase, and the discard phase. Each phase serves as a chapter in the narrative, revealing the true nature of the narcissist and the toll their behaviors can take on the empath.

It's important to remember that this narrative is not set in stone. You are not destined to remain in this toxic cycle. You can break free, reclaim your self-worth, and foster healthier relationships with self-awareness, support, and the right strategies. But before we dive into these strategies, let's take a moment to reflect on the empath-narcissist dance and what it means for you.

What parts of this dance resonate with your experiences?

How might this understanding empower you in your relationships?

Chapter 4

EMPATHIC BOUNDARIES: BREAKING FREE

4

Maybe you are in a relationship with a narcissist and are wondering, is it that bad, really?

Should I let go?

If you are asking yourself these questions, let me give you my backstory of what pushed me to break free.

I had given up everything for Joshua. I sacrificed my own career to build his own. I studied for him, wrote essays, and aced his classes so he could pass and get his degree while my own grades were going downhill. I had this deep belief that we would get married eventually, so I thought all the sacrifices were worth it.

But, after realizing that Joshua was cheating with several women, I decided to leave him. Then, with him on his knees and with tears in his eyes, begging me to take him back, I caved. I was young and naïve, and he had completely hooked me in.

We got back together for about a year before finding out he was cheating on me again. But this time, it was with his own cousin! All these years, I had my suspicions, but I thought that I shouldn't be jealous because, come on, they are family. They actually look alike, so I somehow doubted my own suspicions.

But then the evidence became overwhelming, and I decided to confront them. As you would have guessed, they denied it and told me I was crazy. Joshua always had a way to make everything feel like it was my fault. He told me that I was too sensitive and crazy to think that he could date his own cousin.

It got to a point where I started believing that I was out of my mind. If you combine that with him making me feel worthless and underserving of his love, I can honestly say that my mental health was in jeopardy.

Then, one time, I saw them going out to dinner together, and I texted him. His response was a callous, "Get the F out of my life."

Previously, I hadn't realized that I was an empath. Any negative energy that comes my way, I take it in as if it is my own, so I kept blaming myself for everything he did wrong. It went downhill until I hit rock bottom and tried to take my own life.

Luckily, I survived, and from that moment, I made the conscious decision to get out of his life, let go, and move to another town. I knew that if I stayed, he would do anything within his power to get me back. But my biggest mistake was not healing before jumping into a new relationship. This is a common mistake that most of us make, and if you haven't healed yet, you'll go into a new relationship and project this baggage into it. In the relationships I got in post-Joshua, I ended up hurting not just myself but also the people around me.

As a result, none of those relationships lasted very long. I had unwittingly carried the weight of toxicity for 10 years. This baggage wasn't just emotional; it was a tangled mess of fears – fear of abandonment, fear of intimacy, fear of trust, and the haunting feeling of not being worthy. I figured that if I wanted to get into a healthy relationship, I needed to heal first.

It wasn't until later that I discovered that I was an empath. I had this uncanny ability to read into the emotions of others the moment I stepped into a room. Yet, this blessing was also a curse. I found myself absorbing the energy of those around me, leading to a rollercoaster of emotions in a span of moments.

Sure, it took me a decade to zero in on my identity, but it can never be too late to rebuild your self-worth. A couple of years ago, I made a bold decision to hit pause on dating altogether. This marked the start of my journey into self-reflection and self-love.

During this time, I discovered the unexpected joy of being alone and cultivated a newfound love for books. It was through this that I learned about Empath vs. Narcissistic relationships – something I've been through and overcome.

In this chapter, we will explore the importance of setting boundaries, especially for empaths, since your heightened sensitivity makes you more susceptible to emotional exhaustion and manipulation. Your situation doesn't need to get to the point mine did, and the earlier you break free, the better.

We will examine the role of boundaries in maintaining emotional health, ensuring personal freedom, improving relationships, and preserving self-identity. Let's dive into the first aspect.

4.1 The Importance of Setting Boundaries

Emotional Health

A garden needs a fence to protect it from pests and other threats. Likewise, your emotional health needs boundaries to shield it from negativity and stress. As an empath, you may naturally absorb the emotions of others, which can sometimes lead to emotional overload. By setting clear boundaries, you can control what you let in, ensuring that you're not taking on more than you can handle.

If you've ever felt drained after spending time with a particular person, perhaps a colleague who continually vented about their problems, you have lived your emotional health being impacted by the absence of boundaries. Setting boundaries in this scenario—for example, limiting the time you spend listening to this colleague's complaints—can protect your emotional well-being.

Personal Freedom

When walking a dog on a leash, the leash restricts the dog's movement, preventing it from venturing too far. Now, consider that without some form of control, your time and energy may be like an unleashed dog—scattered in all directions, leaving you feeling stretched thin. Boundaries act like a leash, providing the freedom to explore while ensuring you don't lose yourself in the process.

Contemplate your daily routine. Without boundaries, you may find yourself constantly catering to others' needs and demands, leaving little time for self-care and personal interests. By setting boundaries, you can assure dedicated 'me time', providing the freedom to engage in self-care activities, pursue hobbies, or simply unwind.

Improved Relationships

Visualize a game of soccer. Without markings to define the field and goal areas, the game would be chaotic.

Similarly, relationships without boundaries can become confusing and fraught with misunderstandings. Clear boundaries can help improve relationships by clarifying expectations and preventing misunderstandings.

For example, you may have a friend who frequently cancels plans at the last minute, leaving you feeling disappointed. You can attempt to foster the relationship by setting a boundary, such as expressing how this behavior affects you and suggesting a solution, e.g., asking for a heads-up if they are unsure whether they can commit to your plans.

Self-Identity Preservation

As an empath, it's easy to get so caught up in other people's emotions and needs that you lose sight of your own. Boundaries can help you stay true to your values and needs, preserving your own sense of self.

Let's say you're someone who values honesty, but you have a friend who often lies about small things. While it might seem insignificant, it's still a discrepancy with your values. By setting a boundary, such as expressing that honesty is important to you and that you're uncomfortable with untruths, you're preserving your self-identity.

In conclusion, boundaries are much like a compass, guiding you safely through the dynamic landscape of emotional interactions. They provide a sense of security and control, allowing you to interact with others in a healthy, balanced manner. Setting boundaries is not about isolating yourself from others; it's about creating a safe space for meaningful, positive interactions as well as respecting your needs and teaching others to do the same. So, look upon those boundaries as your emotional safety net, your personal compass. Embrace them, and watch how they transform your empathic experiences.

4.2 Strategies for Establishing Boundaries

Just as an architect uses a blueprint to design a sturdy and functional building, you can use certain strategies to build strong and effective boundaries.

These strategies, while simple, require practice and consistency to implement effectively. Let's explore four key strategies that can help you establish boundaries: clear communication, consistency, self-awareness, and assertiveness training.

Clear Communication

Clear communication is the cornerstone of establishing boundaries. It involves explicitly expressing your needs and limits to others. Say you have a friend who often calls late at night, affecting your sleep. Instead of hoping they'll get the hint when you don't answer, try clearly communicating your boundary—"I value our conversations, but I can't take calls after 10 p.m. as it disrupts my sleep. Can we talk during the day instead?"

The same applies to narcissistic relationships. Be clear about not wanting further communication if you've decided to let go – "I would appreciate it if you no longer contacted me. I am choosing to step away from our connection, and I need you to respect this."

And while narcissists are relentless and will want to push your boundaries, don't be afraid of using the "block" button.

Consistency

Toddlers are constantly testing their boundaries. If they're allowed to stay up late one night but are scolded for the same thing the next night, they'll be confused. Similarly, inconsistency in maintaining boundaries can lead to confusion and weaken their effectiveness.

Being consistent means upholding your boundaries, even when it's difficult. It's about sending a steady message that your boundaries are not negotiable. Let's go back to the friend who calls late at night. If you've communicated your boundary but answered their late-night call because you feel bad, you're sending mixed signals. Consistency is key in reinforcing and maintaining your boundaries.

This is especially true in breaking ties with a narcissist – keep those boundaries steady. One crack, and they are back in your life like they never left.

Self-Awareness

Self-awareness involves checking in with yourself and recognizing when you're feeling drained, upset, or uncomfortable. These feelings can be signals that your boundaries are being crossed.

For example, if you notice you're feeling exhausted after spending time with a particular group of friends, it might be time to set a boundary around the time and energy you invest in those social interactions.

Assertiveness Training

Assertiveness involves standing up for your rights and needs in a manner that respects the rights and needs of others. It involves expressing yourself confidently, using "I"-statements to communicate how you feel and what you need. For example, "I feel overwhelmed when I have too much on my plate. I need to focus on my own tasks and won't be able to help with the project."

Whether it's through a professional course, self-help book, or online resources, assertiveness training can help you build the skills necessary to express your boundaries confidently and effectively.

Building boundaries is much like building a muscle. It requires consistent practice. It might feel uncomfortable at first. But just as regular exercise strengthens muscles, using these strategies consistently can help you build strong and effective boundaries.

So, equip yourself with the strategies of clear communication, consistency, self-awareness, and assertiveness, and start building your emotional safety net. With time and practice, you'll become adept at setting and maintaining boundaries, fostering healthier and more balanced relationships.

4.3 Maintaining Boundaries with Narcissists

Navigating a relationship with a narcissist is sometimes akin to walking a tightrope. It's a precarious balance, with the potential for confusion and emotional upheaval. However, armed with the right strategies, you can maintain your balance and protect your emotional well-being.

Let's explore four such strategies: the Gray Rock method, the No Contact rule, seeking professional help, and building a support network.

Gray Rock Method

Visualize a rock—static, unresponsive, and uninteresting. It doesn't react to its surroundings, whether there's a scorching sun or a torrential downpour. The Gray Rock method is about mirroring this unresponsiveness when dealing with narcissists.

Narcissists thrive on drama and emotional reactions, as they provide the attention and control that they crave. The Gray Rock method entails becoming emotionally non-reactive, making yourself as uninteresting as a gray rock. This can help deter narcissists from engaging in manipulative behavior, as they're not receiving the desired emotional reaction.

Say, for instance, that a narcissist is trying to provoke you with hurtful comments. Instead of reacting with anger or distress, you respond in a neutral, uninterested manner, not giving them the emotional response they seek. The intention is not to be rude or dismissive; it is to protect your emotional space.

No-Contact Rule

Imagine you're weeding a garden. You can keep cutting off the tops, but the weeds will continue to grow back until you remove them from the root. The no-contact rule is essentially about uprooting the influence of the narcissist in your life.

The no-contact rule involves severing all ties with the narcissist—no calls, no texts, no social media interaction— to create a distance that allows for emotional healing and recovery, free from the narcissist's manipulation. This worked perfectly for me when it came to breaking ties with Joshua.

While the no-contact rule can be challenging to implement, especially if the narcissist is a family member or co-worker, it is a powerful strategy for breaking free from the toxic dynamics of narcissistic relationships.

Seeking Professional Help

Like the lighthouse guiding ships through treacherous waters, professional help can serve as your guiding light in the tumultuous seas of narcissistic relationships.

Therapists and counselors trained in dealing with narcissistic behavior can provide invaluable support. They can help you understand the patterns of narcissistic behavior, validate your experiences, and equip you with strategies to set and enforce boundaries.

In addition, if a narcissistic relationship has left you with emotional distress or anxiety, a mental health professional can provide appropriate treatment and aid. Remember, reaching out for help is not a sign of weakness, but a step toward regaining control of your emotional well-being.

Support Network

Picture a group of climbers roped together, ascending a mountain. They rely on each other for safety and support, sharing the load and boosting each other's spirits. In the challenging climb of maintaining boundaries with narcissists, a support network serves a similar purpose.

Your support network could include friends, family members, or a support group of individuals who have had similar experiences. They can provide emotional support, a listening ear, or practical advice. They can also offer validation and encouragement, reminding you that you're not alone in your experiences.

In conclusion, maintaining boundaries with narcissists can be a challenging but necessary step in preserving your emotional well-being. Whether it's through the Gray Rock method, the no-contact rule, seeking professional help, or building a support network, you have a toolkit of strategies to protect your emotional space.

Like that tightrope walker, you are not without support. With these strategies, you can maintain balance and walk the tightrope of narcissistic relationships with confidence and control.

4.4 Personal Stories: Boundary Successes and Failures

Let's now turn our attention to some real-life experiences of empaths navigating their boundaries. These stories spotlight the challenges and triumphs faced by empaths in their pursuit of setting and maintaining boundaries, particularly in situations involving narcissistic individuals.

The Empath's Work Boundary Triumph

Laura is a highly sensitive empath working in a busy and energetic corporate office. She often found herself overwhelmed by the high-pressure environment and the emotions of her stressed colleagues. She frequently ended up absorbing her colleagues' workloads, unable to say no to their requests for help.

One day, Laura decided to set a boundary. She communicated to her team that while she was happy to assist when she could, she could no longer take on additional tasks beyond her capacity. She made it clear that her decision was not out of unwillingness to help but a need to manage her workload effectively.

Laura's decision was met with mixed reactions. Some respected her boundary, while others tried to push against it. Despite the pushback, Laura remained consistent, reinforcing her boundaries when needed. Over time, her colleagues began to respect her limits, and Laura noticed a significant improvement in her work-life balance and emotional well-being.

The Empath's Struggle with a Narcissistic Partner

Next up is the case of Sam, an empath who found himself in a relationship with a narcissistic partner, Amy. Amy was initially charming and attentive, but as the relationship progressed, Sam was on an emotional roller coaster. Amy often belittled Sam's feelings, manipulated him with guilt trips, and demanded constant attention.

Sam attempted to establish boundaries with Amy, expressing his discomfort with her behaviors. However, Amy reacted with dismissal and further manipulation, making Sam question his feelings and needs.

Despite his struggle, Sam's experience with Amy was a wake-up call. He realized the importance of setting and enforcing boundaries, even when met with resistance. Sam's journey with Amy led him to seek professional help, where he learned more about narcissistic behaviors and strategies to protect his emotional well-being.

The Empath's Success with the No-Contact Rule

Finally, we have Emily, an empath who found herself entangled in a relationship with the manipulative narcissist Jake. Emily endured months of emotional turmoil before she established that she'd had enough.

Emily decided to implement the no-contact rule, severing all connections with Jake. She blocked his number, removed him from her social media accounts, and avoided common hangouts.

Jake attempted to regain contact through mutual friends and even showed up at Emily's workplace. However, Emily stood her ground, refusing to engage with him.

Over time, Jake's attempts to reconnect became less frequent, and Emily started to heal from the emotional trauma of the relationship. The no-contact rule turned out to be a crucial boundary that facilitated Emily's recovery and emotional independence.

These three stories illustrate different outcomes of setting boundaries as an empath. Laura found success in setting boundaries at work, while Sam struggled in the face of his narcissistic partner's manipulation, and Emily successfully used the no-contact rule to break free from a toxic relationship.

These diverse experiences underscore the journey to establishing and maintaining boundaries that are unique to each empath. There might be victories, as in the case of Laura and Emily, but there might also be struggles, as with Sam. The crucial thing to remember is that each step taken to establish a boundary, regardless of the outcome, is a step toward protecting your emotional well-being.

As we've seen, boundaries serve as the empath's safety net, providing protection, personal freedom, and improved relationships. While setting and maintaining boundaries can be challenging, especially in interactions with narcissists, it's a crucial aspect of self-care for empaths.

As we continue to explore the fascinating world of empaths and narcissists, keep in mind these personal stories we cover. They remind us that setting boundaries is not only necessary but also possible. So, let's continue our exploration, confident that we can protect our

emotional space and pave the way for healthier
relationships.

Chapter 5

THE SILENT AILMENT: UNDERSTANDING EMPATHIC BURNOUT

5

The heightened sensitivity to emotional and sensory stimuli that defines empaths can often lead to what is known as empathic burnout, a state of physical, emotional, and mental exhaustion caused by chronic stress and overstimulation. Let's uncover the details of this silent ailment, its signs, and its impact.

5.1 Understanding Empathic Burnout

Emotional Overload

Empaths absorb and process the emotions of others in addition to their own. This can lead to an overflow of feelings, creating a sense of emotional congestion. It's like trying to listen to multiple radio stations at once; the resulting noise is loud, chaotic, and confusing. Emotional overload can be a significant contributor to empathic burnout.

Chronic Fatigue

Remember the last time you pulled an all-nighter? Your body felt heavy, your mind foggy, your energy levels depleted. Can you imagine feeling like that most of the time? Because that is often the reality for empaths experiencing burnout.

Chronic fatigue goes beyond the typical tiredness we all get after a long day; it's a persistent sense of exhaustion that doesn't go away with rest, and it's the body's way of signaling that it's been under stress for too long. For empaths, this stress often stems from the continual processing and absorbing of emotional and sensory stimuli.

Loss of Enthusiasm

Think back to a time when you were really excited about something—a new hobby, a project, a trip. Now, imagine that excitement fading away, a sense of indifference taking its place. The feeling is a common sign of empathic burnout.

Activities or hobbies that once brought joy no longer seem appealing. Socializing might feel like a chore. Even simple daily tasks might require a significant effort. This loss of enthusiasm or pleasure in activities you once enjoyed is known as anhedonia, a characteristic symptom of burnout or depression.

Physical Symptoms

Empathic burnout can manifest in various physical symptoms, including headaches, digestive issues, muscle tension, and sleep disturbances. You might find yourself frequently catching colds or struggling with unexplained aches and pains.

These physical symptoms are just like the check engine light in your car that warns you of potential issues; it's your body's way of telling you that something's off, that your body is under too much stress and needs attention.

In conclusion, empathic burnout is a significant concern for many empaths. The chronic emotional overload, coupled with physical fatigue, loss of enthusiasm, and physical symptoms, can significantly impact your quality of life. Recognizing these signs is the first step toward addressing the issue. In the next section, we'll explore strategies to protect your energy and prevent empathic burnout. But for now, take a moment to reflect.

Do any of these signs resonate with you?

Do you think you have ever, or are, experiencing empathetic burnout?

Remember, acknowledging the problem is the first step toward finding a solution.

5.2 Strategies for Energy Protection

Grounding Techniques

Picture yourself standing barefoot on a warm sandy beach, the gentle waves lapping at your feet. Feel the firmness of the earth beneath you, grounding you, connecting you. Grounding techniques work on a similar principle, as they're about establishing a connection with the earth, which should bring you back to the here and now, steadying you amidst the emotional turbulence.

For an empath, grounding techniques can be a powerful tool to dispel emotional overload and regain equilibrium. Simple activities like gardening, walking barefoot on grass, and even hugging a tree or visualizing roots extending from your feet deep into the earth can create a sense of grounding. The techniques can help you release excess emotional energy, and bring you back to your center.

Energy Shield Visualization

Imagine you're inside a bubble, a protective shield that separates you from the outside world. The bubble is clear and permeable, allowing you to observe and interact with the world, yet it keeps you safeguarded. Energy shield visualization is a technique where you imagine yourself surrounded by a protective energy shield, much like that bubble.

This shield acts as a barrier, protecting you from negative energy and emotional overload. It allows you to interact with others without absorbing their emotions. Visualize this shield around you, especially during interactions that you anticipate might be emotionally draining. Over time, this imagined shield can create a psychological buffer, helping you maintain your emotional balance.

Regular Alone Time

Think about the last time you had some alone time, with no tasks to attend to, no people to cater to. How did it feel? Refreshing, relaxing, rejuvenating? Alone time can be a sanctuary for empaths, a safe space to retreat to and recharge.

Regular alone time allows you to relax, process your emotions, and replenish your emotional energy. It gives you space to breathe, to just be. Whether it's a quiet walk in the park, a relaxing bath, or a few moments of silence in the early morning, try to carve out some alone time in your daily routine. It can significantly help in preventing empathic burnout.

Nature Immersion

Ever noticed how a walk in the woods or a day at the beach lifts your spirits and calms your mind? Nature has a therapeutic effect, and for empaths, this can be particularly beneficial. Immersing yourself in nature can help you release accumulated emotional energy and regain your sense of balance.

Whether it's gardening, hiking, birdwatching, or simply sitting in a park, make it a point to spend time in nature regularly. Feel the wind, listen to the birds, soak in the greenery. As you connect with nature, you disconnect from emotional overload, giving your system a much-needed reset.

In essence, protecting your energy is about creating a buffer, a safe space between you and the emotional stimuli around you. It's about learning to manage your unique sensitivity without getting overwhelmed.

As you practice these strategies—grounding techniques, energy shield visualization, regular alone time, and nature immersion—you'll find that your capacity to handle emotional stimuli improves. You'll find yourself becoming more resilient, more balanced, and more in control. So, give these strategies a try and discover the difference they can make.

5.3 Self-Care Rituals for Empaths

Mindful Meditation

Just as a quiet corner at a bustling party offers a breather, mindful meditation can give you a mental respite during emotional turbulence. The practice of mindful meditation involves bringing your attention to the present moment observing your thoughts, feelings, and bodily sensations without judgment.

Mindfulness practice can be particularly beneficial for an empath, as it trains the mind to observe emotions without getting entangled in them. It can be a safe harbor, providing a sense of calm amidst the sea of emotions.

To practice mindful meditation:

i). Find a quiet and comfortable space.

ii). Sit in a relaxed position, close your eyes, and slowly bring your attention to your breathing.

iii).   As you breathe in and out, observe how your body feels, and how your mind reacts.

iv).   If your mind starts to wander, gently bring it back to focusing on your breath.

By making mindful meditation a part of your daily routine, you can strengthen your emotional resilience, improve your ability to manage stress and enhance your overall well-being.

Regular Exercise

Physical activity, whether it's a brisk walk, a yoga session, or a dance class, stimulates the production of endorphins. Endorphins are the body's natural mood lifters, and their release can help reduce feelings of anxiety and depression, improve sleep, and boost self-esteem.

For an empath, regular exercise can be a powerful self-care ritual. It provides a healthy outlet to release emotional overload, making you feel refreshed and revitalized. Thirty minutes a day is all you need to experience the amazing benefits of exercise.

So, lace up those sneakers, roll out that yoga mat, turn on the music, and get moving!

Healthy Eating

For empaths, maintaining a balanced diet can play a crucial role in managing emotional and physical well-being. The right nutrients can help keep your energy levels stable, your mood balanced, and your mind sharp.

A balanced diet should include a variety of foods, providing a mix of carbohydrates, proteins, fats, and a multitude of vitamins and minerals. Hydration is also key, as it contributes to maintaining overall bodily functions and aiding in emotional regulation.

While it's important to enjoy your food, implementing mindfulness and focusing on being mindful of what and how you eat can make a big difference. So, the next time you sit down for a meal, take a moment to appreciate the nourishment you're providing your body. Remember, healthy eating is not just about the food on your plate, but also how you think about food.

Artistic Expression

Whether it's painting, writing, playing an instrument, or crafting, artistic activities can help empaths explore and express their feelings. It's not about creating a masterpiece, but rather about the process of creation itself; it's about letting your emotions guide your creativity, allowing them to take form in your art.

Incorporating artistic expression into your self-care routine can offer a sense of relief and satisfaction. It's like having a conversation with yourself, a dialogue expressed in colors, words, or melodies. So pick up that brush, that pen, that guitar, and let your emotions flow.

Through mindful meditation, regular exercise, healthy eating, and artistic expression, you can nurture your well-being, enhancing your resilience and vibrancy.

Each self-care ritual is a step toward managing empathic burnout and maintaining emotional equilibrium. They're not just activities; they're acts of self-love and self-preservation, and they're about listening to your needs and taking steps to fulfill them. So, as you navigate life as an empath, remember to take care of yourself. You are worth it.

The only question is, what's your preferred self-care ritual?

5.4 Personal Stories: Empathic Self-care Successes

Below are some real-life stories on how different empaths employed the above-stated strategies for self-care.

Story of an Empath's Daily Meditation Routine

Meet Daisy, an empath with a heart that feels deeply and a mind that absorbs emotions like a sponge. The constant influx of emotions, both her own and those of others, used to leave Daisy feeling worn out. She'd feel like a ship adrift in a turbulent sea of emotions, struggling to stay afloat.

Then, Daisy discovered meditation. She started with just five minutes a day, sitting quietly and focusing on her breath. Gradually, she increased her meditation time, incorporating mindfulness techniques to stay grounded in the present moment.

Meditation became Daisy's daily anchor, a ritual that helped her start the day with a sense of calm and balance. For her, it was like finding a lighthouse amidst the emotional storm, guiding her safely through the waves. Daisy's story underlines how a simple daily routine of mindful meditation can become a powerful self-care tool for empaths.

Story of an Empath's Journey to Physical Fitness

Next up is Jack, an empath who often felt physically drained due to his high sensitivity to others' emotions.

Jack's body seemed to carry the weight of all the emotions he absorbed, causing him to feel exhausted and lethargic.

One day, Jack decided to make a change. He started with a simple workout routine, just a few minutes of exercise every day. Over time, Jack expanded his routine, adding different forms of exercise like jogging, weightlifting, and yoga.

Regular exercise became a game-changer for Jack. It was like a daily energy boost, revitalizing him physically and emotionally. It wasn't just about building physical strength but also about releasing the accumulated emotional energy. Jack's transformation signifies the potent impact of regular exercise on an empath's physical and emotional well-being.

Story of an Empath's Artistic Outlet for Emotional Release

Finally, there's Maria, an empath with a creative soul. Maria's heightened emotional sensitivity often felt to her like a whirlwind of feelings. She was looking for a way to express these emotions, a way to transform the emotional whirlwind into something beautiful.

Maria found her outlet in art. She started painting, letting her emotions guide every brush stroke. Each emotion took on a life of its own on the canvas, transforming it from an abstract feeling into a tangible form.

Art became Maria's sanctuary, a space where she could express her emotions freely, without judgment or restraint. Each piece of art was a reflection of her emotional state, a visual diary of her empathic experiences. Maria's story is a testament to the therapeutic potential of artistic expression for empaths.

The experiences of Daisy, Jack, and Maria highlight the transformative power of self-care in managing empathic sensitivities. They remind us that self-care isn't an indulgence, but a necessity for empaths. Their stories inspire us to prioritize our own well-being, to create our own daily rituals of self-care. After all, it's only when we take care of ourselves that we can truly embrace our empathic abilities and use them to enrich our lives and the lives of those around us.

In the next chapter, we will shift our focus to the emotional aspects of being an empath. The emotions we feel are a core part of our human experience. For empaths, these emotions are amplified, making emotional wellness a crucial aspect of their lives. So, let's continue exploring the remarkable world of empaths, understanding their unique challenges, and discovering strategies to foster their emotional wellness.

Chapter 6

EMPATHY AND EMOTIONAL WELLNESS: NAVIGATING THE EMOTIONAL LANDSCAPE

6

Every emotion, whether your own or others', is like a pebble that ripples across your emotional landscape. These ripples can either enhance their emotional wellness or lead to emotional turmoil.

In this chapter, we'll explore the connection between empathy and emotional health and the ways you can navigate your emotional landscape to foster emotional wellness.

6.1 The Connection between Empathy and Emotional Health

Empathy as a Tool for Emotional Understanding

When you watch a movie, you often find yourself sharing the characters' emotions, feeling their joy, their sadness, and their fear. This ability to understand and share another's feelings is the essence of empathy. For empaths, this emotional resonance is heightened, allowing you to tune into others' feelings with remarkable depth and clarity.

Empathy can be a powerful tool for emotional understanding. Empathy helps you connect with others on a deeper level, fostering more meaningful relationships. It can also enhance your self-awareness, as understanding others' emotions can provide insights into your own.

For instance, if you find yourself feeling anxious after speaking with a worried friend, it's not just their worry you're feeling; it's also a reflection of your own susceptibility to anxiety. Recognizing this can help you address your own emotional needs and foster emotional wellness.

The Role of Empathy in Emotional Regulation

When you're in tune with your emotions, you're better equipped to manage them. You can recognize when an emotion is building up and can take steps to address it before it becomes overwhelming. This is particularly crucial for empaths, who can experience emotions more intensely due to their heightened sensitivity.

For example, if you're feeling increasingly stressed as a work deadline approaches, recognizing this early on can allow you to implement stress management strategies, like taking short breaks, practicing deep breathing, or even seeking support from a colleague.

Emotional Contagion: The Downside of Empathy

Now, imagine being in a room where everyone starts yawning. Before long, you'll likely find yourself yawning, too. This is a simple example of emotional contagion, the phenomenon where we 'catch' the emotions of those around us. For empaths, this emotional contagion is more intense and can be a downside of heightened empathy.

Being susceptible to emotional contagion means that negative emotions, like stress or anger, can easily rub off on you, leading to emotional distress. It's like walking on a tightrope, where the slightest breeze can cause you to lose your balance. However, being aware of this susceptibility can help you take steps to protect your emotional balance.

For instance, if you have a colleague who often vents about their problems, you might find yourself feeling stressed or anxious after talking to them. Recognizing this emotional contagion allows you to set boundaries, such as limiting the time you spend listening to them or practicing grounding techniques after your interactions.

6.2 Empaths and Mental Health Support

The Role of Therapy in Emotional Wellness

As an empath, you might find yourself feeling like a ship in a storm, tossed around by the waves of emotions. Therapy can serve as your anchor, offering stability and guidance.

In therapy, you have the opportunity to explore your emotional experiences in a safe and supportive environment. Therapists can provide valuable insight into the nature of empathy and how it impacts emotional health. They can help you understand you unique emotional responses and develop strategies to manage them effectively.

Therapy can also assist you in dealing with the challenges that often accompany your heightened sensitivity, such as emotional overload, difficulty setting boundaries, and susceptibility to emotional contagion. Therapists can equip you with tools to protect your emotional well-being, such as grounding techniques, mindfulness practices, and self-care strategies.

Moreover, therapy can be a platform for you to explore your feelings of empathy in depth. It can help you understand the positive aspects of your empathic abilities, such as deep emotional understanding and connection with others, as well as the potential for emotional healing.

Support Groups and Community for Empaths

If you've ever been part of a team working toward a common goal, you know how reassuring it can be to know you're not alone. The companionship, the shared experiences, the mutual support—they all add up to make the journey easier and more rewarding.

Support groups offer a similar sense of community for empaths. In these groups, you can connect with others who share your experiences and challenges. You can learn from each other, share coping strategies, and offer mutual support.

Being part of a community of empaths can also help alleviate feelings of isolation that you may often experience due to heightened sensitivity. It can provide a sense of belonging and understanding that can be immensely comforting.

Support groups can take various forms: offline groups that meet in person or online communities where members connect virtually; formal groups facilitated by a mental health professional; or informal communities brought together by shared experiences. Regardless of the format, the essence of support groups lies in mutual understanding, shared learning, and collective growth.

Online Resources for Emotional Support

In today's digital age, help is often just a click away. The internet is a treasure trove of resources for empaths seeking emotional support. From informative articles and self-help blogs to online forums and social media groups, there's a wealth of information and support available online.

Online resources can provide valuable insights into the experiences and challenges of empaths. They can offer tips and strategies to manage emotional overload, set boundaries, and foster emotional wellness. They can also link you to professional resources, such as therapists and counselors who specialize in working with empaths.

Moreover, online platforms can serve as a space for you to share your experiences and connect with others who understand your unique challenges. You can participate in discussions, ask questions, and offer support to others. It's like having a global support group at your fingertips.

However, while online resources can be incredibly helpful, it's important to approach them with discernment. Not all information found online is reliable or accurate, and what works for one person may not work for another. It's essential to consider the source of the information and to consult a mental health professional if needed.

In conclusion, mental health support plays a pivotal role in fostering emotional wellness for empaths. Whether it's through therapy, support groups, or online resources, you can find the help and guidance you need to navigate your emotional landscape effectively.

Remember, you don't have to navigate these waters alone. Reach out, seek support, and embrace the journey toward emotional wellness. You are an empath, and that is your superpower. So, let's continue exploring this superpower to understand its nuances, challenges, and potential and learn, grow, and embrace the empath within.

6.3 Personal Stories: Empaths and Emotional Wellness

As always, I use real-life examples with the teachings in this book to drive the point home.

Overcoming Emotional Burnout: A Personal Journey

Consider the tale of Danielle, an empath who found herself grappling with emotional burnout. With her heightened sensitivity, Danielle had always resonated deeply with the emotions of those around her. But over time, the continuous onslaught of emotional stimuli began taking its toll.

Danielle noticed she was constantly tired, had lost interest in activities she used to enjoy, and was struggling with persistent headaches. She felt like a phone with too many apps open, her battery draining faster than it could recharge.

Upon realizing that she was facing empathic burnout, Danielle decided to take action. She began incorporating mindfulness practices into her daily routine, spending a few minutes each day focusing on her breath, bringing herself back to the present moment. She also started setting aside time each day for activities that she enjoyed, like painting and gardening.

Gradually, Danielle began to see changes. She felt less tired, her headaches reduced, and she found herself enjoying her hobbies again. It was as if she had found a hidden power bank, providing her with the extra charge she needed. Danielle's story is a testament to the power of recognizing and addressing empathic burnout.

Finding Emotional Balance: An Empath's Story

Now, Ethan is an empath who always felt like he was on an emotional roller coaster, as with most empaths. Ethan's heightened empathy meant he not only experienced his own emotions intensely, but also picked up on the feelings of those around him. The result was a rowdy mix of emotions that often left him feeling unbalanced and overwhelmed.

Ethan decided to seek therapy to help him manage his emotional landscape. His therapist introduced him to the concept of emotional grounding and taught him techniques to help him stay centered amidst emotional turbulence.

Ethan started practicing these techniques, focusing on his breath when he felt overwhelmed and consciously connecting with his physical surroundings to anchor himself in the present moment. Over time, Ethan noticed that he was better able to handle emotional stimuli without getting swept up in them.

Ethan's experience shows us that, with the right tools and support, empaths can find their emotional balance, turning the roller coaster ride into a smoother journey.

The stories of Danielle and Ethan shed light on the unique challenges empaths face in maintaining emotional wellness. Each story is a beacon of hope, showing that empaths can navigate their emotional landscapes effectively with awareness, determination, and the right strategies. These stories remind us that being an empath is not a burden but a gift that, when managed well, can lead to a rich and fulfilling emotional life.

As we move forward, let's carry these stories and draw inspiration from them. Let's remember that, as empaths, we have the power not only to feel deeply but also to transform these feelings into a source of strength and growth.

So, let's turn the page and learn how you can navigate romantic relationships healthily as an empath.

Chapter 7

EMPATHS IN LOVE: NAVIGATING THE EMOTIONAL TIDES OF ROMANTIC RELATIONSHIPS

7

Love: it's a powerful force, capable of lifting us to the highest peaks of joy but also plunging us into the deepest valleys of despair. For empaths, who feel emotions most intensely, the experience of love is a wild ride filled with exhilarating highs and heart-wrenching lows.

As an empath, you might face unique challenges in romantic relationships stemming from your heightened sensitivity. But remember, these challenges do not define you; they are merely stepping stones on your path to finding balance and fulfillment in love.

7.1 Empaths and Romantic Relationships

The Challenges of Being an Empath in Love

Think about the last time you saw a romantic movie. Remember the emotional intensity, the heart-tugging moments that made you laugh, cry, or sigh with longing. Being an empath in love can feel a lot like being inside that movie, with all the emotional intensity magnified tenfold.

One of the main challenges empaths face in relationships is the **tendency to absorb their partner's emotions.** This can lead to emotional overload, leaving you feeling drained or overwhelmed. Imagine being a sponge, soaking up not only your emotions but also those of your partner. It's like carrying two emotional backpacks, making the journey of love much more strenuous.

Another challenge for empaths is the **struggle to establish emotional boundaries.** As an empath, you naturally gravitate toward helping and healing others.

However, in a romantic relationship, this can lead to a blurred line between helping and enabling, between understanding and losing your identity. It's like being a lighthouse, guiding your partner through their emotional storms, but risking your own stability in the process.

The Beauty of Deep Emotional Connections

Empaths have a unique ability to profoundly understand and connect with their partner's emotions. This can lead to deep emotional intimacy, strengthening the bond between you and your partner. It's like having a secret language, a heart-to-heart connection that transcends words.

Moreover, empaths' natural caring and nurturing nature can bring a lot of warmth and understanding to a relationship. Your ability to empathize with your partner's feelings can make them feel seen, heard, and valued.

Empaths and the Fear of Emotional Intimacy

Have you ever stood at the edge of a diving board, feeling both excitement and fear at the prospect of the plunge? That's what the fear of emotional intimacy can feel like for empaths. While you crave the deep connection, the vulnerability it requires can be daunting.

As an empath, you might fear losing your identity in the relationship, given your tendency to absorb your partner's emotions. The thought of opening up and letting someone else into your emotional world can feel threatening, maybe stirring up fears of rejection or misunderstanding.

This fear of emotional intimacy can hold you back from forming meaningful relationships. It's like standing on that diving board forever, too scared to take the plunge and experience the exhilarating swim. However, with awareness and courage, you can overcome this fear, opening yourself up to the joy of deep, emotional intimacy.

In essence, being an empath in love can be a journey of contrasts—the joy of deep connections, the pain of emotional overload, the fear of intimacy, and the beauty of shared emotions. It's a dance, a melody of love played on the strings of empathy. And like any dance, it becomes more graceful with practice and understanding. So, embrace the dance, my dear empath. Step onto the dance floor of love with courage and grace, while the melody of empathy guides your steps.

7.2 Strategies for Healthy Relationships

Communication Techniques for Empaths

For empaths, effective communication is crucial. Due to your heightened sensitivity, you may pick up on unspoken emotions or undertones that others may miss.

On the one hand, it can be a strength, as it allows you to understand your partner more deeply. On the other hand, it can lead to misunderstandings if you misinterpret the subtle cues.

Here are a few techniques to enhance your communication skills:

- **Expressive Speaking:** As an empath, you're adept at understanding emotions. Use that ability to clearly and assertively express your feelings and needs. Use "I" statements to express your feelings rather than blaming or criticizing your partner.

- **Active Listening:** This involves fully focusing on your partner when they're speaking, acknowledging their feelings, and responding thoughtfully. It shows your partner that you value their feelings and views.

- **Non-Verbal Communication:** Pay attention to your body language, facial expressions, and tone of voice. They often convey more than words.

Remember, communication is a two-way street. It is not just about expressing your feelings and needs but also understanding and respecting your partner's feelings and needs.

Setting Healthy Boundaries in Relationships

Picture a beautiful garden, enclosed within a protective fence. The fence not only defines the garden's boundaries but also protects it from outside intruders. In relationships, boundaries serve a similar purpose. They define each partner's emotional territory and protect it from invasion or neglect.

Whether you are in a relationship with a narcissist or not, setting boundaries in any relationship is crucial. For empaths, this can be particularly challenging. Your natural inclination to help and heal can make it hard to say "no" when you need to. But without boundaries, you risk depleting your emotional energy, leading to resentment and burnout.

Here are some tips to help you set healthy boundaries:

- **Identify Your Limits:** Understand what you're comfortable with and what drains you emotionally. Your limits might be defined in terms of time, emotional energy, personal space, or social interactions.

- **Communicate clearly:** Once you've identified your limits, communicate them clearly to your partner. Be assertive, but respectful. Remember, your needs are equally as important as your partner's.

- **Stick to Your Boundaries:** It's not enough to set the boundaries; you also need to maintain them. If your partner oversteps a boundary, remind them of it and discuss how you can avoid such instances in the future.

Creating healthy boundaries doesn't restrict your relationship. Instead, it acts as a framework where your relationship can grow and flourish without draining your emotional energy.

Nurturing Emotional Independence in a Relationship

For empaths, maintaining emotional independence in a relationship can be a delicate balancing act. Given your capacity to deeply resonate with your partner's emotions, you might sometimes lose touch with your own.

Here are a few strategies to nurture emotional independence:

- **Prioritize Self-Care:** Regularly spend time nurturing your own emotional health. Engage in activities that you enjoy, and that replenish your emotional energy.

- **Encourage Mutual Respect**: Ensure that your relationship is a space where both you and your partner's emotions and needs are acknowledged and respected.

- **Develop Your Interests:** Have hobbies and interests outside of the relationship. This not only enriches your life but also ensures that your happiness doesn't solely depend on your relationship.

Emotional independence doesn't mean distancing yourself from your partner. Rather, it's about ensuring that while your lives are intertwined, they're not tangled. You are two individuals in love, each whole and fulfilled, sharing a journey together.

In conclusion, being an empath in a relationship can be a journey of self-discovery. At the end of the day, it is important to learn to balance your empathy with your personal needs, to communicate effectively, to set healthy boundaries, and to nurture your emotional independence while also nurturing your bond with your partner. Above all, embrace your empathic abilities and use them to create a relationship that is not only loving but also emotionally balanced and fulfilling.

7.3 Empaths and Non-Narcissistic Partners

Recognizing Healthy vs. Toxic Traits in Partners

Healthy traits in a partner include respect, honesty, open communication, emotional availability, and independence. A partner demonstrating these traits will value your feelings, respect your boundaries, communicate openly, and maintain their individuality while cherishing the bond you share.

In contrast, toxic traits include manipulation, gaslighting, emotional unavailability, excessive criticism, and disrespect. Partners with these traits can drain your emotional energy, disregard your feelings, and potentially lead to emotional distress.

As an empath, your ability to tune into emotions can act as a radar, helping you distinguish between healthy and toxic traits in a partner. Trust your intuition, take note of any red flags, and remember that everyone deserves to be in a relationship that nurtures and respects them.

The Dynamics of an Empath-Non-Empath Relationship

In an empath-non-empath relationship, your emotional sensitivity meets the non-empath's emotional stability. This can create a balance, with you, the empath, bringing depth of understanding and the non-empath providing grounding energy.

However, it's vital for both partners to understand and respect each other's emotional capacities. You should realize that your partner may not experience emotions as intensely. Conversely, the non-empath needs to appreciate your emotional depth, without feeling overwhelmed or pressurized to reciprocate at the same level.

This understanding can create a harmonious relationship where each partner is playing their part, contributing to a healthy, beautiful relationship.

The Benefits of a Balanced Relationship

In a balanced relationship, both partners' needs and feelings are valued and met. The give-and-take is equal, and mutual respect is the norm. For an empath, a balanced relationship offers the space to express empathy while also prioritizing self-care.

A balanced relationship with a non-narcissistic partner can provide stability, understanding, and mutual growth. Like a safe harbor, it's a place where you can be your authentic self, without fear of emotional manipulation or overload.

In conclusion, being an empath in a relationship does not mean losing yourself in your partner's emotions.

Ideally, you'd want to create a harmonious duet where you can resonate with your partner's feelings while maintaining your emotional melody.

Also, to recognize healthy traits in your partner, understand the dynamics of your relationship, and strive for balance. So, as an empath, step into the dance of love with awareness and confidence. You have the emotional depth and resilience to navigate the tides of romance and create a harmonious, balanced, and deeply fulfilling relationship.

7.4 Personal Stories: Empaths in Love

From Emotional Overwhelm to Balanced Love: A Personal Journey

Meet Olivia, an empath who was in a whirlwind of emotions when she fell in love with her college sweetheart, Brad. With her heightened ability to sense emotions, Olivia found herself deeply affected by every nuance of Brad's feelings. She ended up carrying not only her own emotions but also Brad's, leading to a state of constant emotional overwhelm.

Olivia's deep love for Brad and her desire for a healthier emotional state propelled her to seek change. She began practicing mindfulness, grounding herself in her own emotions rather than being swept away by Brad's. She also started setting aside time daily for self-care, doing things that brought her joy and relaxation.

Over time, Olivia noticed a shift: she was better able to manage her emotions, and her relationship with Brad began to feel less overwhelming and more balanced. Olivia's story highlights the power of mindfulness and self-care in transforming love from an emotionally overwhelming experience to a balanced and fulfilling one.

The Power of Boundaries: An Empath's Love Story

Now, let's turn our attention to Adam, an empath who was in a relationship with a demanding partner. Brittney constantly sought Adam's attention and validation, leaving him emotionally drained. Due to his empathic nature, Adam found it hard to say "no" to Brittney and often neglected his own needs to cater to hers.

Realizing that this pattern was detrimental to his well-being, Adam decided to set boundaries in his relationship. He communicated his needs to Brittney, expressing the importance of having time and emotional space for himself. Initially, Brittney struggled to understand Adam's need for boundaries, but over time, she came to respect them.

Setting boundaries transformed Adam's relationship with Brittney. It created a healthier dynamic where Adam could care for Brittney without neglecting his own emotional well-being. This tale of Adam and

Brittney underscores the power of boundaries in fostering healthier and more balanced relationships for empaths.

Finding Love Beyond Narcissism: An Empath's Transformation

Finally, let's explore the transformation of Sydney, an empath who found herself in a toxic relationship with a narcissist. Sydney was initially drawn to Adrian's charisma and charm, but over time, she received Adrian's manipulation and criticism. Being an empath, Sydney was deeply affected by Adrian's negative emotions and found herself in a state of constant emotional turmoil.

Recognizing that the relationship was causing her harm, Sydney gathered the courage to break free from Adrian's control. She sought therapy, where she learned about narcissism and the manipulative tactics employed by narcissists.

Empowered with this knowledge, Sydney began her healing process. She focused on self-care, spent time with supportive friends, and joined a support group for survivors of narcissistic abuse. Over time, Sydney regained her emotional strength and found love again, this time with a partner who respected and valued her empathic nature.

Sydney's transformation sends a powerful message that leaving a narcissistic relationship can be the beginning of a journey toward self-discovery, healing, and finding healthier love.

In romance, being an empath can feel like a dance, a beautiful yet complex choreography of emotions. The stories of Olivia, Adam, and Sydney remind us that although the dance may be challenging, with self-awareness, self-care, and resilience, empaths can navigate the rhythm of romance. As you continue your dance, let their experiences inspire you, their resilience empower you, and their transformations remind you of the beautiful potential within your empathic nature.

In the next chapter, we will delve into another aspect of an empath's life, where their heightened sensitivity interacts with the professional world.

Chapter 8

EMPATHS AT WORK: CHANNELING SENSITIVITY INTO SUCCESS

8

Imagine standing in front of a mirror and seeing not just your reflection but also the reflections of those around you. As an empath, you often serve as such a mirror in your social and professional interactions, reflecting and absorbing the emotions of those around you.

While this heightened sensitivity can be challenging, especially in a professional setting, it can also be harnessed as a powerful asset. This chapter will explore how you, as an empath, can navigate the workplace and leverage your empathic abilities for success.

8.1 Empaths in the Workplace

The Challenges of Being an Empath in a Professional Setting

For an empath, stepping into a bustling workplace can feel like walking into a storm. The myriad of emotions swirling around the office—stress, excitement, frustration, joy—can all come rushing toward you, leaving you feeling overwhelmed and drained.

You might find yourself absorbing a colleague's stress over a tight deadline or a manager's frustration with a project's progress. You may feel emotionally exhausted after a day of meetings, having absorbed the varied feelings of your team members. This constant emotional influx can lead to burnout, affecting your well-being and productivity.

The Strengths of Empaths in Team Dynamics

Imagine a team where everyone truly understands and values each other's feelings, where communication is empathetic, and where conflicts are resolved with understanding and respect. Doesn't that sound like a dream team? Well, as an empath, you have the potential to contribute significantly to creating such a team dynamic.

Your ability to sense and understand your team members' emotions can foster better communication and collaboration. You can sense underlying tensions and address them before they escalate into conflicts. You can provide emotional support to team members going through a tough time, improving team morale. In essence, your empathic abilities can act as a glue, binding the team together and enhancing its overall performance.

Empaths and Leadership Roles

Think about a leader you truly admire. What makes them stand out? Is it their strategic vision, their decision-making skills, or perhaps their ability to connect with their team on a human level? If you're leaning toward the latter, you're not alone; empathetic leadership is increasingly being recognized as a key factor in organizational success.

As an empath, your natural inclination toward understanding and caring for others can make you a highly effective leader. Your team members are likely to feel valued and understood, leading to increased motivation and productivity. You can sense the team's morale and take proactive measures to boost it when needed. Your deep understanding of your team's emotions can also guide you in making decisions that consider not just business objectives but the team's emotional well-being.

So, while being an empath can present unique hardships in the workplace, it also brings a host of strengths. The key lies in managing the challenges effectively while leveraging your strengths.

In the following sections, we'll delve into strategies that can help you do just that. So, buckle up and get ready to transform your professional life as an empath!

8.2 Strategies for Workplace Success as an Empath

Self-Care Strategies for the Workplace

As an empath, it's not unusual to absorb the emotional energies in your surroundings, and the work environment is no different. That's why it's crucial to have a toolkit of self-care strategies specifically tailored for the workplace. By practicing self-care at work, you can protect your emotional health and ensure you're performing at your best.

One of the first things to consider is your physical work environment. You may find that you're particularly sensitive to harsh lighting, loud noises, or even the energy of the people around you. If possible, try to create a workspace that feels calming and comfortable. This could mean bringing in a desk lamp with softer lighting, using noise-canceling headphones, or decorating your space with plants or personal items that bring you joy.

Taking regular breaks throughout the day can also help prevent emotional overload. Use these breaks to step outside and get some fresh air, do a quick mindfulness exercise, or simply relax and recharge. Even a few minutes away from your desk can make a big difference.

Remember, it's okay to set boundaries at work. If you find certain tasks or interactions particularly draining, look for ways to manage these situations. This might involve delegating tasks, if possible, or scheduling challenging meetings at the time of day when you feel most energized.

Navigating Workplace Politics as an Empath

Workplace politics can be a tricky terrain for anyone, but even more so for empaths. The undercurrents of emotion, hidden agendas, and power plays can all be overwhelming for someone who feels emotions so deeply. But don't worry; there are ways you can navigate workplace politics without sacrificing your empathic nature.

One strategy is to practice emotional detachment. It means observing the emotions and dynamics around you without absorbing them—being present and aware but not getting emotionally involved. Think of it like being a duck in the rain: let the water (or, in this case, the emotions) roll off your back.

Another strategy is to strengthen your assertiveness skills. Assertive communication involves expressing your thoughts, feelings and needs in an open and respectful manner. As an empath, you might struggle with assertiveness, especially if you're worried about causing upset or discord. However, remember that your feelings and needs are just as important as anyone else's.

Finally, try not to take things personally. This can be hard for empaths, who naturally empathize with others and may internalize their emotions or actions. Most of the time, though, people's actions are about them and not you.

Leveraging Empathic Abilities for Career Success

Being an empath in the workplace is not just about managing challenges but also about leveraging your empathic abilities to excel in your career. Your ability to understand and connect with others can be a significant asset in many professional scenarios.

For instance, if you work in a team, your ability to sense the emotions and dynamics within the group can help facilitate better communication and collaboration. You can anticipate potential conflicts and address them before they escalate. You can also provide support and understanding to your colleagues, boosting team morale and productivity.

Your empathic abilities can help you lead with compassion and understanding in leadership roles. You can understand your team members' motivations and challenges, and provide support and guidance tailored to their needs. This can lead to a more motivated and engaged team, and ultimately, better results.

In customer-facing roles, your ability to empathize with people can help you provide exceptional service. You can understand the customer's needs and concerns on a deeper level, and tailor your service accordingly. This can lead to higher customer satisfaction and loyalty.

In essence, being an empath in the workplace is about balancing self-care with service to others. It's about navigating the emotional landscape of the workplace, while also leveraging your empathic abilities for career success. While the path may sometimes be challenging, remember that your empathy is a strength and not a weakness. In fact, it's a tool that can help you create not just a successful career, but also a fulfilling one.

8.3 Empaths and Career Choices

Ideal Careers for Empaths

Empaths, with their ability to understand and connect with others' emotions, are often naturally drawn to careers that involve helping others. Fields such as **counseling, social work, and healthcare** are usually fulfilling for empaths, as they provide an opportunity to use their empathy to support and heal.

Creative careers may also be a great fit for empaths. Whether it's **writing, art, music, or design,** these fields allow empaths to express their emotions and experiences in a creative form, offering a therapeutic outlet for their intense feelings.

Teaching and mentoring roles may be rewarding for empaths as well. The ability to understand and connect with students on an emotional level can enhance the learning experience, making it more engaging and meaningful.

The key to choosing the right career as an empath lies in understanding your unique strengths and interests. Ideally, you'll find a path that not only utilizes your empathic abilities but also brings you joy and fulfillment.

The Role of Empathy in Different Professions

If you aren't in any of the above-mentioned professions, don't worry. Empathy can go a long way in different professions, as stated below.

In the **healthcare** profession, empathy can enhance patient care, making patients feel understood and supported. It can build trust, improve communication, and potentially lead to better health outcomes.

In **business and leadership** roles, empathy can foster a more positive and productive work environment.

Leaders who understand their team members' feelings and perspectives can make more informed decisions, resolve conflicts effectively, and boost team morale.

In **customer service** roles, empathy can lead to more satisfying customer experiences. Understanding a customer's needs and concerns can help provide better service and foster customer loyalty.

Even in professions where empathy might not seem central, such as **engineering or finance**, it can enhance teamwork, communication, and problem-solving. By understanding their colleagues' perspectives, engineers can collaborate more effectively, and finance professionals can better meet their clients' needs.

In essence, empathy is like a universal key, unlocking doors across various professions. It's a soft skill that can enhance hard results, contributing to individual and organizational success.

Empaths as Entrepreneurs

For empaths, entrepreneurship can offer a unique opportunity to shape a business that aligns with their values and leverages their empathic abilities. As an empath entrepreneur, you can create a work environment that values emotional well-being, fosters open communication, and prioritizes meaningful work.

Your ability to understand your customers' needs and perspectives can guide your business decisions, leading to products or services that truly resonate with your target audience. Your empathic nature can also help you build strong relationships with customers, partners, and employees.

However, entrepreneurship also comes with challenges. It requires a balance of empathy and assertiveness, of emotional understanding and strategic thinking. As an empath entrepreneur, self-care should be a priority, to ensure that the demands of running a business don't lead to emotional burnout.

Ultimately, being an empath can add a unique dimension to your career, whether you choose a traditional profession or the path of entrepreneurship. The key lies in understanding your empathic nature and finding ways to incorporate it into your work life. It's about transforming your empathy from a challenge into a strength, a tool that can guide you toward a fulfilling and successful career.

8.4 Personal Stories: Thriving Empaths at Work

From Overwhelm to Success: An Empath's Career Journey

Meet Henrietta, a social worker, and an empath. Early in her career, Henrietta found herself constantly absorbing the emotional turmoil of her clients. Each day felt like an emotional marathon, leaving her drained and overwhelmed. She loved her job, but was on the verge of burnout.

One day, Henrietta decided to make a change. She started practicing mindfulness, focusing on her own emotions rather than absorbing those of her clients. She also started setting aside time each day for self-care activities that she enjoyed, like painting and yoga.

Slowly but surely, Henrietta began to see a shift. She was better equipped to manage her emotions, and her work no longer left her feeling overwhelmed. The journey wasn't easy, but Henrietta had transformed her sensitivity into a strength, using it to connect with her clients while also taking care of her emotional health.

The Power of Empathy in Leadership: A Personal Story

Next, let's look at the story of Max, a team leader in a tech company and an empath. Max's ability to understand his team members' emotions and perspectives made him a beloved leader. However, he often found himself taking on the emotional burdens of his team, which took a toll on his own emotional health.

Recognizing the need for balance, Max began implementing emotional boundaries. He started by communicating his needs to his team and encouraging them to do the same. He also made a point of practicing self-care, ensuring he had time to recharge outside of work.

The results were transformative. Not only did Max's emotional health improve, but the overall team dynamic also became more positive and productive. Max's story shows us that empathy when balanced with self-care and boundaries, can be a powerful tool in leadership.

Finding the Right Career as an Empath: A Personal Transformation

Finally, let's explore the transformation of Lola, a graphic designer, and an empath. Lola's heightened sensitivity made her an exceptional designer, able to intuit clients' needs and translate them into stunning visuals. However, the high-stress environment of her corporate job left her feeling emotionally depleted.

Seeking a change, Lola decided to start her own graphic design business. As an entrepreneur, Lola was able to create a work environment that catered to her empathic nature. She set her own pace, chose projects that resonated with her, and built strong relationships with her clients.

Lola's career transformation was about more than changing jobs; it was about aligning her work with her empathic nature. Today, Lola is not just a successful entrepreneur, but also a happier, more balanced individual.

The stories of Henrietta, Max, and Lola highlight the unique challenges and opportunities empaths face in the workplace. They remind us that while being an empath at work may sometimes feel like a struggle, it can become a strength with the right strategies and mindset. They inspire us to embrace our empathy, to care for ourselves as we care for others, and to seek balance in our professional lives.

As we wrap up this chapter, let's remember that our empathy is not a burden we carry to work each day, but a gift we bring. It's a tool we can use to build stronger relationships, better understand our colleagues and clients, and create a work environment that values emotional well-being.

In the next and final chapter, we'll dive into one of the most crucial aspects of being an empath: personal growth.

Chapter 9

YOUR JOURNEY TO PERSONAL GROWTH AND TRANSFORMATION

9

9.1 Empaths and Personal Transformation

Think back to a time when you walked into a room and immediately sensed the mood. Or perhaps, recall a moment when you felt someone else's joy or pain so deeply as if it were your own. These experiences, common for empaths, are your emotional superpowers.

However, as we have established, they can often leave you feeling overwhelmed or misunderstood. This is where the journey of self-discovery begins, which is all about embracing and understanding your empathic abilities, and learning to navigate them in a way that empowers rather than drains you.

A significant part of this journey involves self-reflection. Ask yourself,

How does being an empath affect your daily life?

How does it impact your relationships, your work, your well-being?

Reflecting on these questions can provide valuable insights into your unique experiences as an empath and lay the foundation for your personal transformation.

The Role of Empathy in Personal Growth

Empathy is more than just feeling what others feel; it's a bridge to understanding, a path that connects you to others on a deep emotional level. This understanding can be a powerful catalyst for personal growth.

For example, imagine you're at a friend's house, and they're upset about a recent breakup. Your empathic abilities allow you to sense their pain, but it's what you do with this understanding that contributes to your personal growth. You could use it to offer comfort, to provide a listening ear, or to give advice. Each of these actions not only helps your friend but also fosters qualities like compassion, patience, and kindness within you.

Empathy can also enhance self-awareness, as understanding others' emotions can provide insights into your own. It's like looking into a mirror, seeing not just your reflection but also gaining a deeper understanding of yourself.

Transforming Sensitivity into Strength

As an empath, you've likely been told that you're "too sensitive," as if sensitivity is a weakness.

But what if you could transform this sensitivity into strength?

What if you could channel your empathic abilities into something empowering?

One way to do this is by using your sensitivity to foster deeper connections with people. Your ability to understand and share others' feelings can make you a great friend, partner, or leader. It can open doors to professions where empathy is a key strength, like counseling, healthcare, or social work.

Another way is to use your empathy for creative expression. Many empaths are drawn to the arts, where they can express their deep emotional world through writing, painting, music, or dance.

Finally, being sensitive also means being in tune with your own emotions, which can be a powerful tool for personal growth. It can guide you toward self-awareness, helping you recognize and acknowledge your feelings, needs, and boundaries.

To conclude this section, your journey as an empath is about more than just navigating the challenges of high sensitivity. First, it's about leveraging this sensitivity for personal growth and transformation. Second, it's about turning the mirror inward, understanding your empathic abilities, and using them as a tool to foster personal growth. Third, it's about transforming sensitivity into strength, turning empathy into empowerment.

9.2 Strategies for Empathic Empowerment

Techniques for Harnessing Empathic Abilities

Balancing Empathy with Self-Care: As an empath, it's easy to get swept away in the emotional currents of those around you. Learning to balance your empathy with self-care is crucial for maintaining your emotional health.

This might involve setting aside time each day for activities that bring you joy, grounding exercises to center your emotions, or simply saying "no" when you need to.

Practicing Mindful Empathy: Mindful empathy involves being present and aware of the emotions you're experiencing, whether they're your own or others'. It involves observing these emotions without judgment or absorption.

Practicing mindful empathy can help you better manage your empathic abilities, which reduces emotional overload and enhances your emotional understanding.

The Role of Mindfulness in Empathic Empowerment

Picture a tranquil lake, its surface perfectly reflecting the sky above. This serene stillness is the essence of mindfulness—for empaths, it can be a powerful tool in managing your empathic abilities.

Mindfulness involves being fully present in the moment, observing your thoughts and feelings without judgment. For empaths, mindfulness can provide a much-needed anchor in the sea of emotions. By focusing on the present moment, you can prevent yourself from getting swept away by the emotional undercurrents around you.

Mindfulness can also enhance your empathic abilities, allowing you to observe emotions—both yours and those of others—with greater clarity and understanding. It's like cleaning the lens of your emotional glasses, allowing you to see the emotional landscape around you more clearly.

There are various ways to cultivate mindfulness, such as practicing meditation, engaging in mindful activities like yoga or nature walks, or simply taking a few moments each day to focus on your breath. By integrating mindfulness into your daily routine, you can better manage your empathic abilities, transforming them from a source of overwhelm into a tool for personal growth and empowerment.

Building Resilience as an Empath

Think of a tree, standing tall and sturdy against the wind. Despite the force of the wind, the tree stands firm, bending but not breaking. This is resilience, and for empaths, building resilience is key to managing your empathic abilities.

Resilience involves the ability to cope with stress and adversity to bounce back from difficult experiences. For empaths, who often face emotional overload due to their heightened sensitivity, building resilience can provide a buffer against emotional exhaustion.

As you build this resilience, remember that the purpose of it is to help protect you from emotional exhaustion. So, as you cultivate mental resilience, you should have this goal at the back of your mind.

Building resilience as an empath can involve several strategies:

- **Developing a Strong Support Network:** Having people you can rely on for emotional support can help you navigate difficult emotional experiences. This might involve reaching out to trusted friends or family members, joining a support group, or seeking professional help.

- **Practicing Self-Care**: Regular self-care can help replenish your emotional energy, boosting your resilience against stress and emotional overload. This might mean taking time each day to relax and do things you enjoy, eating a healthy diet, getting regular exercise, or practicing good sleep habits.

- **Fostering a Positive Mindset:** Maintaining a positive outlook can help you cope with emotional challenges more effectively. This might mean practicing gratitude, focusing on your strengths rather than your weaknesses, or reframing negative experiences in a more positive light.

By building resilience, you can navigate the emotional waves with greater ease and harness your empathic abilities without getting swept away. Like the tree standing firm against the wind, you too can stand firm amidst the emotional winds, bending but not breaking, growing stronger with each gust.

9.3 Empaths and the Journey of Self-Discovery

The Role of Intuition in Self-Discovery

Intuition, often dubbed "the sixth sense," is your subconscious mind communicating with you. It's that gut feeling that alerts you when something is off or the inner voice that encourages you when you're on the right track.

To tap into your intuition,

i).   Start by quieting your mind. In the hustle and bustle of daily life, your intuitive voice can get drowned out by the noise.

ii).   Take a few moments each day to sit in silence to tune into your intuition.

iii).   Practices like meditation, mindful breathing, or time spent in nature can also create the space for your intuition to be heard.

Listening to your intuition can provide valuable insight into your true self. It can help you recognize patterns, understand your emotional triggers, and identify your needs and desires. It's like having a personal guide on your journey of self-discovery, pointing you toward the truths that lie within you.

The Power of Self-Acceptance for Empaths

Self-acceptance is about acknowledging your strengths and weaknesses, successes and failures, and emotions and experiences without judgment or criticism. It's about embracing your empathic nature with its gifts and challenges.

As an empath, self-acceptance can be particularly empowering. Self-acceptance encourages you to embrace your sensitivity rather than see it as a burden. Moreover, it empowers you to honor your emotional needs and set boundaries. Self-acceptance provides the foundation for self-love and self-care, both of which are essential elements of your emotional well-being.

To cultivate self-acceptance, start by becoming more self-aware. Notice your thoughts, feelings, and reactions—without judgment. Practice self-compassion and treat yourself with the same kindness and understanding you'd offer a dear friend. Celebrate your successes, no matter how small, and view your failures as opportunities for growth and learning.

Empaths and the Quest for Authenticity

Authenticity is about being true to your feelings, beliefs, and values. It's about expressing yourself honestly and openly, without fear of judgment or rejection. For empaths, authenticity involves honoring your emotional sensitivity and expressing your emotions freely and honestly.

To cultivate authenticity, it's important to understand and accept your empathic nature. Recognize your emotional patterns, identify your values, and honor your emotional needs. Practice expressing your feelings and needs openly and assertively. Don't be afraid to set boundaries to protect your emotional well-being.

In your quest for authenticity, always keep in mind that it's okay to be different. As an empath, you experience the world in a way that others may not understand, and that's okay. Your unique perspective is a gift, not a flaw. Embrace it, celebrate it, and most importantly, be true to it.

It's important not to forget that your journey of self-discovery as an empath is a personal and ongoing process. In addition to tuning into your intuition, embracing self-acceptance, and striving for authenticity, it's about discovering who you truly are—beyond the labels and expectations—and embracing your unique path. As you continue on this journey, remember that you are not alone. On the contrary, you are part of a community of empaths, each on their own journey of self-discovery. So, keep exploring, keep growing, and most importantly, keep being you.

9.4 Personal Stories: Empaths and Personal Growth

Embracing Sensitivity: An Empath's Journey to Self-Acceptance

Meet Amelia. Her life as an empath was akin to walking on a tightrope, teetering between emotional overload and her deep desire to help others. Amelia's sensitivity was often perceived as a weakness, a trait that made her "too emotional" or "too soft." She found herself constantly trying to fit into a mold, suppressing her sensitivity to navigate her relationships and work life.

However, a chance encounter with a book about empaths sparked a change. Amelia began to see her sensitivity not as a weakness but as a unique strength, a trait that allowed her to connect with others deeply. She began to accept herself as an empath, embracing her sensitivity rather than hiding it.

This self-acceptance was liberating. It was as if a weight was lifted, freeing her to be her authentic self. Today, Amelia stands tall as an empath, her sensitivity shining as her superpower.

From Overwhelm to Empowerment: An Empath's Transformation

Next, let's look at the case of Jerry, an empath who often found himself emotionally drained and overwhelmed. As a school counselor, Jerry was constantly exposed to a whirlwind of emotions from his students. The intense absorption of these emotions left him feeling exhausted, leading him to question his ability to continue in his profession.

A turning point arrived when Jerry attended a workshop on empath empowerment. Guided by the strategies he learned, Jerry began to practice emotional grounding techniques. He also set boundaries with his students, ensuring he could provide support without depleting his emotional energy. As he implemented these changes, Jerry noticed a shift: he felt less overwhelmed and more in control of his emotional landscape.

Today, Jerry continues to thrive in the role of a counselor, where his empathic abilities allow him to make a difference in his students' lives. His story demonstrates the power of empathic empowerment, a symbol of the transformation from emotional overwhelm to strength and success.

The Power of Authenticity: An Empath's Personal Growth Story

Finally, the story of Ciara, an empath who transformed her life through the power of authenticity. For most of her life, Ciara felt like she was wearing a mask, hiding her true self to fit into societal norms. As an empath, she felt things deeply but often suppressed her emotions for fear of being judged or misunderstood.

One day, Ciara decided to remove her mask and embrace her authentic self. She began to express her emotions openly, setting boundaries in her relationships and prioritizing her emotional well-being. As she embraced her authenticity, Ciara felt a profound sense of freedom and self-acceptance. She no longer needed to hide her sensitivity; instead, she celebrated it.

Ciara's transformation is a testament to the power of authenticity. Indeed, it sends a powerful message to empaths everywhere: the message that being true to yourself is not just liberating but also a crucial step toward personal growth.

These stories of Amelia, Jerry, and Ciara shine a light on the unique paths to personal growth as an empath. They remind us that being an empath is not a burden, but a gift. When embraced and managed effectively, this gift can lead to profound personal transformation. So, dear empath, remember that your sensitivity is your strength, and your empathy is your superpower. Use them wisely;

use them proudly, and watch as they guide you toward personal growth and fulfillment.

CONCLUSION

Conclusion

As we reach the end of our shared journey, it's time to pause, reflect, and gather the pearls of wisdom we've uncovered along the way.

Key Takeaways: Empaths, Narcissists, and You

Together, we've delved deep into the realms of empaths and narcissists, uncovering their unique traits and understanding their contrasting dynamics. You've discovered what it means to be an empath with your heightened sensitivity and your profound emotional understanding.

You've explored the world of narcissists, their need for admiration, and their lack of empathy. And most importantly, you've begun the process of finding your own place within this dynamic.

Your Journey Forward: Using What You've Learned

The knowledge you've gotten on this journey goes beyond theory; it represents a practical toolkit, a collection of strategies and insights that can serve as resources for navigating your relationships and life. Whether you find yourself as an empath facing the overwhelming emotions of others or dealing with a narcissist in your life, keep in mind the invaluable strategies we've explored.

Use them as your guiding compass, helping you to navigate through intricate situations and make informed choices. And if you're on a path of personal growth to overcome narcissistic traits, you've now equipped yourself with fundamental tools for healing and transformation.

Final Thoughts: Finding Balance in a World of Extremes

In a world that often values toughness over sensitivity and assertiveness over empathy, finding balance can be challenging. But remember that it is not about changing who you are to fit into the world; it is about finding your balance within it.

This includes setting boundaries to protect your emotional well-being, cultivating resilience and practicing self-care, and celebrating your sensitivity and using it as a tool for connection, understanding, and growth.

The Path Forward: Embracing Your Empathic Gifts

Now, while my book ends here, your journey is just beginning. As you continue forward, don't forget to embrace your empathic talents wholeheartedly. Utilize them to enhance both your life and the lives of those you meet.

Always keep in mind that you're not walking this path alone. You are part of a community composed of empaths and individuals with narcissistic traits, each embarking on their own voyage of healing.

Share Your Thoughts

Dear Readers,

I am writing to express my deepest gratitude for your support in reading my book. Your time and engagement mean the world to me. If you've enjoyed the journey through these pages, please consider leaving a review. Your words can guide and inspire other readers, helping them discover the book and decide if it's the right fit for them.

Reviews are the lifeblood of independent authors, and your honest feedback can make a significant impact. Thank you for being a part of my literary journey, and I look forward to hearing from you.

To submit a review, kindly navigate to your Order History, locate the book in your purchased items, and select 'Write a Product Review.'

With gratitude,

Joyce T.

Bonus Gift

As a modest gesture to express my gratitude, I'm offering you a complimentary of my bundle e-book that delves into the topic of narcissism, providing deeper insights and practical strategies for healing from its root causes to the core:

Healing Haven 2-in-1 Bundle
Highly Sensitive Empath vs. Narcissistic Individual Unveiled + The Narcissist's Journey to Healing:

A Comprehensive Guide to Recognize, Navigate, and Flourish in Relationships with these Contrasting Personalities

Scan QR code to download with Access Code: healing

<u>www.JoyceTbooks.com</u>

References

- *5 Big Challenges Empaths Face In Romantic Relationships + How To Overcome Them* https://www.mindbodygreen.com/articles/problems-empaths-have-in-relationships

- *5 Protection Strategies for Empaths* https://drjudithorloff.com/5-protection-strategies-for-empaths/

- *5 Scientific Explanations of Empathy and Empaths* https://chopra.com/articles/5-scientific-explanations-of-empathy-and-empaths

- *9 Narcissistic Manipulation Tactics & How to Deal* https://www.choosingtherapy.com/narcissistic-manipulation-tactics/

- *9 Ways to Rebuild Self-Esteem After a Toxic Relationship* https://seattlechristiancounseling.com/articles/9-ways-to-rebuild-self-esteem-after-a-toxic-relationship

- *14 Types of Narcissism & What to Know About Them* https://www.choosingtherapy.com/types-of-narcissism/

- *15 Signs You Might Be an Empath* https://www.healthline.com/health/what-is-an-empath

- *15 Tips for Setting Boundaries With a Narcissist* https://www.choosingtherapy.com/setting-boundaries-with-a-narcissist/

- *20 empathic person traits to improve workplace culture* https://uk.indeed.com/career-advice/career-development/empathic-person-traits

- *20 Ideal Careers for Empaths (With Salary Info)*
  https://www.indeed.com/career-advice/finding-a-job/careers-for-empaths

- *20 Self-Care Ideas for Highly Sensitive People*
  https://highlysensitiverefuge.com/self-care-ideas-for-highly-sensitive-people/

- *50 Ways To Ground Yourself As An Empath*
  https://enlightenedempathy.wordpress.com/2018/02/12/50-ways-to-ground-yourself-as-an-empath/

- *A Spiritual Perspective on the Highly Sensitive Person*
  https://www.highlysensitivehumans.com/post/a-spiritual-perspective-on-the-highly-sensitive-person

- *Beyond Thick Skin: A Story of Empathy, Strength, and Personal Growth*
  https://medium.com/@thepowertoact327/beyo

nd-thick-skin-a-story-of-empathy-strength-and-personal-growth-23a8a75e0a9

- *Burnout in Sensitive People: Empath Burnout, Shutdown and Compassion Fatigue* https://healyournervoussystem.com/empath-burnout-harness-the-power-of-empathy-without-damaging-your-mental-and-physical-health/

- Effect of Mindfulness on Empathy and Self-Compassion: ... https://www.ncbi.nlm.nih.gov/pmc/articles/PMC7139462/

- *Empathy Burnout: What It Is & How to Cope* https://www.choosingtherapy.com/empathy-burnout/

- Empathy in narcissistic personality disorder: from clinical and empirical perspectives https://pubmed.ncbi.nlm.nih.gov/24512457/

- *Empathy Is a Rare and Valuable Strength in the Workforce* https://highlysensitiverefuge.com/empathy-rare-and-valuable-strength-in-the-workforce/

- *Empathy Is The Most Important Leadership Skill According To Research* https://www.forbes.com/sites/tracybrower/2021/09/19/empathy-is-the-most-important-leadership-skill-according-to-research/

- *Five Signs That A Relationship Might Be Toxic* https://www.betterhelp.com/advice/relations/5-ways-to-distinguish-toxic-relationships-from-healthy-ones/

- *How I'm Letting Myself Mourn a Lifetime of Narcissistic Abuse* https://medium.com/fearless-she-wrote/how-im-letting-myself-mourn-a-lifetime-of-narcissistic-abuse-177ad61b1144

- *The Long-Term Effects of Narcissistic Abuse* https://www.charliehealth.com/post/the-long-term-effects-of-narcissistic-abuse

- How Many Types of Empaths Are There? Here Are Our Favorite 14 https://greatist.com/happiness/types-of-empaths

- *Empathy Burnout: What It Is & How to Cope* https://www.choosingtherapy.com/empathy-burnout/

- *You're not crazy. You're an empath.* https://janellecepero.com/blog/whats-an-empath

- *How to Cope With Being an Empath, According to Experts* https://www.realsimple.com/health/mind-mood/emotional-health/being-an-empath

- *50 Ways To Ground Yourself As An Empath*

  https://enlightenedempathy.wordpress.com/2018/02/12/50-ways-to-ground-yourself-as-an-empath/

- How to Improve Your Empathic Listening Skills: 7 Techniques

  https://positivepsychology.com/empathic-listening/

- *How to Stop Being a Narcissist: 21 Tips*

  https://www.choosingtherapy.com/how-to-stop-being-a-narcissist/

- Living with pathological narcissism: a qualitative study

  https://www.ncbi.nlm.nih.gov/pmc/articles/PMC7427292/

- *Narcissistic personality disorder [Diagnosis & treatment]*

  https://www.mayoclinic.org/diseases-conditions/narcissistic-personality-disorder/diagnosis-treatment/drc-20366690

- *Narcissistic personality disorder [Symptoms & causes]* https://www.mayoclinic.org/diseases-conditions/narcissistic-personality-disorder/symptoms-causes/syc-20366662

- *Setting Healthy Boundaries in Relationships* https://www.helpguide.org/articles/relationships-communication/setting-healthy-boundaries-in-relationships.htm

- *The Dangerous Relationship Between Empaths & Narcissists* https://www.choosingtherapy.com/empaths-and-narcissists/

- *The Long-Term Effects of Narcissistic Abuse* https://www.charliehealth.com/post/the-long-term-effects-of-narcissistic-abuse

- *The Toxic Relationship Between an Empath and a Narcissist*

  https://www.carlacorelli.com/narcissistic-abuse-recovery/empath-and-narcissist-relationship/

- The Ultimate Guide to Dealing with Narcissists and Protecting Your Emotional Well-being

  https://www.carlacorelli.com/narcissistic-abuse-recovery/dealing-with-narcissists/

- *Therapy for Empaths — Highly Sensitive Person Treatment Options*

  https://www.mentalhelp.net/blogs/therapy-for-empaths-and-highly-sensitive-persons/

- *Treating Survivors of Narcissistic Abuse*

  https://www.psychotherapynetworker.org/article/treating-survivors-narcissistic-abuse

- *What are the long-term effects of gaslighting?*

  https://www.medicalnewstoday.com/articles/long-term-effects-of-gaslighting

- *What Is It Like to Be an Empath? True Stories and Real Life Experiences*

  https://letterpile.com/serializations/What-Is-It-Like-To-Be-An-Empath-True-Stories-and-Real-Life-Experiences-Part-2

- *You're not crazy. You're an empath.*

  https://janellecepero.com/blog/whats-an-empath

- *A Spiritual Perspective on the Highly Sensitive Person*

  https://www.highlysensitivehumans.com/post/a-spiritual-perspective-on-the-highly-sensitive-person